M000011422

The Chase

What are leaders saying about *The Chase-*

The Chase does an excellent job of relating the ideas of success and positive motivation as taught in the Scriptures. Just as the original edition of Success, Motivation, and the Scriptures impacted me as a young leader, so will a new generation of leaders find practical benefits in areas such as vision, faith, and goal-setting.
--JOHN C. MAXWELL, NYT BEST SELLING AUTHOR OF THE 21 IRREFUTABLE LAWS OF LEADERSHIP

In *The Chase*, readers will truly find "the most excellent way" as Bill Cook carefully examines what Scripture teaches and how it applies to our lives today in the areas of success and motivation. This is a must read for followers of Jesus!
--PHYLLIS H. HENDRY, PRESIDENT AND CHIEF EXECUTIVE OFFICER, LEAD LIKE JESUS

This pivotal book has helped bridge the gap in my mind between faith and success. It is a crucial read for anyone desiring to impact others. I have read it several times. Do so and you'll be challenged and encouraged.
--JEREMIE KUBICEK, CEO OF GIANT IMPACT; AUTHOR OF MAKING YOUR LEADERSHIP COME ALIVE.

The Chase is a jewel of a book — a modern classic. In this fresh new edition, Bill Cook has given us biblical principles of success that are practical, encouraging and have stood the test of modern times.
--DAN REILAND, EXECUTIVE PASTOR OF 12STONE CHURCH; AUTHOR OF AMPLIFIED LEADERSHIP

In a world of upside-down living; a place where compromise is common place and the pursuit of prosperity and success eclipses our sensibility, morality and ethics, Dr. Bill Cook gives us strategies for right-side up living within the pages of his book entitled, *The Chase*. Filled with a plethora of practical principles Dr. Bill Cook offers us a go-to manual. A "must-have" library edition, this book is compelling because of its salient features. It is readable, relatable and practical. I believe this book is a timeless classic which should be preserved and left as a legacy for generations to come.
–CINDY TRIMM, BEST SELLING AUTHOR, FOUNDER, TRIMM INT.

The Chase is a book every aspiring leader should read. Literally every aspect of walking with God as a leader of others is addressed in this book. It's a must read if you want to model what Christ taught about leadership and true success in life.
--OS HILLMAN, PRESIDENT, MARKETPLACE LEADERS, AUTHOR TGIF TODAY GOD IS FIRST, AND CHANGE AGENT

Bill Cook's generous use of real life experiences of people in the Bible and modern times helps us grasp concepts that literally guarantee success in life. If *The Chase* became a best seller, it would change everything!
--RICK L STEPHENS, CHAIRMAN, HORIZON HOBBY, INC., FORMER CHAIRMAN, PINNACLE FORUM AMERICA

I can think of very few books which influenced me more as a young pastor than *Success, Motivation, and Scriptures*. *The Chase*, an update edition of this ageless classic, has a powerful message for today's generation. I will recommend it to every young leader I know.
-- JACK GRAHAM, PASTOR, PRESTONWOOD BAPTIST CHURCH

This book is a terrific roadmap for seasoned business people – particularly entrepreneurs – as well as students embarking on their careers.
--Karen Lausten, Founder, PutItTogether.biz

The Chase offers you a fresh and balanced approach to success in your work...and in your life!
--Tom Elliff, President, International Mission Board, SBC

I believe that the best human motivation comes from our Creator and the timeless scriptures we have in our possession. Because it is built from the universal truths of the Bible, The Chase is in many ways timeless. I recommend it to you.
--Tim Elmore, Founder and President of GrowingLeaders.com

You'll find The Chase to be a powerful, life-changing book as you apply its truths.
--Todd Duncan - NYT Best Selling Author of High Trust Selling and Time Traps.

Some books make you look *inward* within yourself. Others make you look *upward* toward God. Yet others make you look *outward* - how to live successful and satisfied lives. This book is sure to challenge you on all three while giving pragmatic steps to achieve your dreams.
--Samuel R. Chand, Author of Cracking Your Church's Culture Code

The Chase provides powerful principles for pursuing and achieving a successful and yet balanced life. If placed into the hands of young adults it will endow them with guiding principles for their future.
--Rita Kiefer Medall - President, Medall Media

This book is a must read for every Christian leader and deserves a spot on the shelf among the Christian classics.
--STAN TOLER, BESTSELLING AUTHOR

The Chase is a classic in every sense of the word! I first read his original book *Success, Motivation, and the Scriptures* when I was in my mid-twenties and it has occupied a special place on my bookshelf ever since. Each year I have re-read the remarkable content in this book and soaked in its Godly wisdom.
--DWIGHT "IKE" REIGHARD, LEAD PASTOR, PIEDMONT CHURCH

Bill Cook does a masterful job of weaving his powerful insights, illustrations and applications into God's timeless Truth. No matter what your age or season of life – this book will leave you fully equipped for success and true fulfillment.
--SUSAN CONLEY, CHRISTIAN PROFESSIONALS WORLDWIDE

I am personally excited and delighted that this book has been updated and republished. To have *The Chase* available to this generation is so right!
--JACK TAYLOR, DIMENSIONS MINISTRIES

Bill Cook has brought back a classic. If you want to be inspired, read *The Chase*... if you want to experience irrefutable success in your life, apply what it says!
--TIM ENOCHS, BUILDING CHAMPIONS COACH, SPEAKER, AUTHOR OF THE STREET SWEEPER

No matter what you are chasing or how far along you are, *The Chase* will give you perspective and encourage you.
--KEN COLEMAN, SYNDICATED RADIO HOST, THE KEN COLEMAN SHOW & AUTHOR OF ONE QUESTION

The Chase will re-frame your thinking about Success and Motivation and leave you panting with exuberance rather than exhaustion.
--RANDY ROSS – SPEAKER, AUTHOR, ENTHUSIASM COACH

Bill Cook's insight into scripture and his ability to apply it to true success in life is a treasure and gift from God to all who will read and heed these words. I recommend *The Chase* with much anticipation and expectation. Read it and reap!
--O.S. HAWKINS, PRESIDENT AND CHIEF EXECUTIVE OFFICER, GUIDESTONE FINANCIAL RESOURCES

The Chase is an excellent read. This book will not fail to enhance one's desire to attain the fullness of life which Jesus has promised us.
--LLOYD G. MINTER, FORMER SR. VICE PRESIDENT/GENERAL COUNSEL/ BOARD OF DIRECTORS, PHILLIPS PETROLEUM CO.

The Chase should be a building block for any leader in business that wants to glorify God by understanding His directives and standards.
--CHRISTY SPEER, CEO, GC&C INVESTMENTS, LLC

I love *The Chase* because it has Leadership, Motivation, Wisdom and Faith in every chapter. Applying the teachings found in this book will allow one to elevate his/her walk with God in their personal and business life.
--LINDA DAVIDSON, SR LOAN OFFICER/ BRANCH MANAGER, SERVICE FIRST MORTGAGE

The Chase, is a very practical and easy read based on biblical principles. We are wise to study these writings and prayerfully consider how the Holy Spirit can apply the words of wisdom to our life. Thank you Bill for being a catalyst for Christ's transforming truth.
--BOYD BAILEY, MINISTRY VENTURES PRESIDENT, WISDOM HUNTERS

The Chase

Success, Motivation and the Scriptures

William H. Cook

worden WA associates

I

www.chasebookonline.com

© Copyright 2012 William H. Cook

All rights reserved. Except as permitted under the U.S. Copyright Act of 1976, no part of this publication may be reproduced, distributed, or transmitted in any form or by any means, or stored in a database or retrieval system, without written permission of the publisher.

Cover Design by Worden Associates

ISBN: 978-0-9856368-0-7
ISBN eBook: 978-0-9856368-1-4
ISBN Audio Book: 978-0-9856368-2-1

Unless otherwise noted, all Scripture quotations are from "NASB" are taken from the New American Standard Bible®, Copyright © 1960, 1962, 1963, 1971, 1972, 1973, 1975, 1977, 1995 by The Lockman Foundation. Used by permission. Scripture quotations marked "KJV" are taken from the Holy Bible, King James Version, Cambridge, 1769. Scripture quotations marked "NIV" are taken from HOLY BIBLE, NEW INTERNATIONAL VERSION®. Copyright © 1973, 1978, 1984 by International Bible Society. Used by permission of Zondervan Publishing House. Scripture quotations marked HCSB are taken from the Holman Christian Standard Bible®, Copyright © 1999, 2000, 2002, 2003, 2009 by Holman Bible Publishers. Used by permission. Holman Christian Standard Bible®, Holman CSB®, and HCSB® are federally registered trademarks of Holman Bible Publishers. Scripture quotations marked "NLT" are taken from the Holy Bible, New Living Translation, copyright © 1996. Used by permission of Tyndale House Publishers, Inc., Wheaton, Illinois 60189. All rights reserved.

Printed in the United States of America

DEDICATION

To these special ones who are
great motivators in my life:

My wonderful wife, Rachel

Our kids and their mates,
Rod and Camille Minor
Craig and Ann Cook
Jim and Pam Moorhead

And our 10 Grandkids

And to all of you special people
who have encouraged me
and prayed for me
along the way

Foreword

While managing my first major market radio station I had a sense that there was something missing between my striving for success and my understanding of what it would look like once I reached the elusive dream of being "successful."

During this phase of my life I discovered the book by Dr. Bill Cook, *Success, Motivation, and the Scriptures*. For the first time I learned that the ideas of positive motivation and success were not only taught in the Bible, but they were available and achievable through the power of God and the work of the Holy Spirit. The chase for success now had meaning!

Success, Motivation, and the Scriptures was first published in 1974. It has been a joy and honor to work with Dr. Cook to update and republish his original book with the new title, *The Chase*. When Dr. Bill Bright, founder of Campus Crusade for Christ read the original manuscript of Dr. Cook's book, he said, "Business people need to be exposed to the many practical benefits in the areas of success, self-image, vision, faith, and goal-setting found in this book." As I work with and mentor young, success-motivated men and women, the need for these biblical principles is abundantly clear today just as it was when this book was written for a baby boomer generation.

May you discover how God fits seemingly opposites together for His glory!

Dennis Worden - Publisher/Editor
Worden Associates
www.goworden.com

Author's Introduction

The chase has intensified. Nearly everyone seems to be involved in some type of chase, chasing after ideas, always hoping the next idea will be the best idea, and the dreams of a lifetime will suddenly be fulfilled.

George Barna, founder of The Barna Research Group, a polling firm that specializes in American church culture and trends, had some interesting words in his 2010 poll about trends. His findings are well worth reading, but I am just pulling a few words from one of his sentences. *"A growing number of people are desirous of learning pragmatic solutions for life."*

Where do we find these practical solutions? Inside each of us is a hunger, sometimes an intense hunger for more out of life. We were born with it. We want to be something special, do something special, reach some goals, achieve, and accomplish something worthwhile. Our desire is that tomorrow we want to be more than we are today. And on the horizon, many are experiencing God-given desires to sacrifice and help others discover and achieve goals God has for them as well.

This book is written with a belief that God also wants elements of exciting success *flowing through* each of us. If that is to happen, ideas must be examined, and special ones pulled together with an outcome of, you guessed it, significance and success.

In the process of working through these ideas, I want to caution you—*don't deify fear*. Be aware of the danger of making a god out of fear! The goals are huge. You will wrestle with ideas—about success, about motivation, about spiritual things. Find the right mix in these fields, and life can be lived to the fullest. But that's the problem with life—finding the right mix.

It is my belief that the individual who correctly assimilates success, motivation, and the truths of Scripture will experience fantastic excitement and achievement. I believe we can each be thankful just for the *privilege* God has given us of being here, and having the opportunity to seek the vision and the plan He has for each of us.

William H Cook, 2012

Dr. William H. Cook has served as Senior Pastor, University Vice-President, Professor, and Motivational Speaker in the U.S. and internationally.

Contents

Part Six: Excitement Plus — The Result Of Proper Motivation

PART ONE:

Problems With Success and Achievement

THE CHASE BEGINS

I like the spirit of the one who goes thru life wanting to stretch. I like the spirit of the motivator who has spent years and brought lots of laughs teaching people how to reach for the top. I like the guy who wears a T-shirt with letters across the front spelling PBPWMGIFWMY and on the back the shirt has the sentence, "Please Be Patient With Me, God Isn't Finished With Me Yet." I like the thrill that comes with believing that there is a plan for every life, goals worth reaching for, and that the human mind is a fantastic gift not yet even close to being fully utilized in any of us.

—William H. Cook

Nate was sitting in his office, frustrated. Inside that multi-storied building, his office was just one of many. It was special. Since signing on with the company fresh-out of college, he had been pleased…, up until now. He had worked hard in his career, and the office he occupied now was more spacious than most.

Nate's name and title on that small plaque on the wall just outside his office was part of what made this office exceptional. In his mind, this was the first title he had been given that really meant something. There were several above him, but this job was a good one. He had lots of reasons to be satisfied; anyone could have told him that. But he wasn't.

He should feel some peace, but all he felt was frustration. And his doctor had recently prescribed some medication for high blood pressure and anxiety attacks.

Bombarded! He sat at his desk thinking, his mind full, flooded with his Twitter account, his Facebook account, his personal e-mail, his business e-mail, searching for time to spend with his wife and kids, plus looking for some inner satisfaction.

Motivation was an important part of Nate's new job assignment, and that really bugged him. He was not good at motivating himself, and now he needed to motivate all those employees working under him in the department.

This very morning, while he was getting ready to go to work, he had wondered, "God, are You interested or not interested in my being successful?"

This afternoon, for some strange reason, he's thinking about his name, Nate. Actually his full name, Nathan. His parents had told him years ago that his name meant "gift from God." But he's feeling like anything but a gift from God right now.

His mind is on a roll. Moving fast. About not only his name, but about some of the personal questions that have come into his mind at different times. His questions are many—about life, about success, about God, about how to put things together and come out ahead.

Like Nate, we all have thoughts of life, of the meaning of life, and putting it all together. Have you ever asked questions like these, or at least wondered about them, like…

• Do I set goals or do I just decide to do what the Bible says and not be anxious about tomorrow?

• One voice tells me I need a self-controlled life, and another says I need a Christ-controlled life—which is right?

• If you ask me, I'm certain I need more confidence, but didn't I read something in the Bible telling me to "place no confidence in the flesh?"

• What if I've really been working on strengthening my self-image, but then I read some words about following Jesus— and I'm supposed to "deny myself?"

• I'm just like most people, and I'm wanting to master positive thinking, but I'm having trouble with eight of the Ten Commandments that begin with negative words like "You shall not….?"

•   How can I strive to be "Number One" and at the same time be humble like the Bible says I'm supposed to be?

Frustrating, isn't it? Just about the time the brain gets loaded with exciting ideas, along comes another idea that seems to be correct, but it also seems to conflict! Those concepts may appear to be exciting but they just don't seem to go together. Any hope here?

There's a battle going on inside the human brain. Lose this battle and your chance of being motivated toward success, achievement and new heights, is off the chart in a downward spiral.

The truth is that while you may be chasing things in many directions, you are also *being* chased. Make a list of what you see or think about, or what you just file away in your brain until you have more time to concentrate. Take a moment and start writing. How much have you fed into your brain's filing cabinet in the last 24 hours? Or, even in the last 7 days?

Could it be a case of "too much?" Maybe even too many good things? Could there just be some time-consuming, schedule-weakening things? Facebook, TV programs, commercials, texting, email, blogs, electronic gadgets, video games—are any of these things chasing you to the point of "too much?" Any room left for personal motivation, face-to-face relationships or anything else to squeeze in there? Could even God get your attention if He wanted to?

The front cover of a Spring 2011 nationwide newsmagazine showed a front view picture of a face. Across the forehead of the person there were two words in giant letters, with a subtitle below:

BRAIN FREEZE[1]
How the Deluge of Information Paralyzes
Our Ability to Make Good Decisions

The Chase

When I opened to page 28 to read the full story, I saw a new headline for the article, and a new subtitle: "I Can't Think"

"The Twitterization of our culture has revolutionized our lives, but with an unintended consequence—our overloaded brains freeze when we have to make decisions."

Imagine! The human brain, the powerful human brain—Stalled! Stopped! Overloaded! Frozen! Can you relate to a time when you felt brain freeze? Maybe it was that time when the ice cream you were eating was too cold, and your brain went numb, at least for the first few bites.

One summer job I had during high school days involved working in the cold storage vault at an ice-cream distribution center while guys on the big trailer truck outside were sending in boxes of ice-cream cartons. The boss knew how long we should stay inside before we came out of the freezer storage room for a break. That's enough memories for me!

Far more serious is the problem mentioned in the "brain freeze" article. The brain-analysis experts are referring to overloading the brain with too many ideas and then keeping it overloaded, until our vital decision-making process is affected.

Success Ideas! Motivation Ideas! Any Brain Room for Those?

It is important that the brain not be frozen with too many ideas, nor be undernourished with too few. Nor do we want our life impacted by wrong ideas, ideas of failure. We all know some who have listened to bad ideas, acted on them, and never quite recovered.

The magazine article about "Brain Freeze" could lead to some thoughts we may need: (1) Sometimes less is more! We may need to focus on both the number and the importance of the things we have our minds chasing. (2) Prioritize! What about both the number and kind of things we are allowing to chase us and fill our minds? Those also cause brain freeze! We determine what we let enter the mind—and how long it gets to stay there. Sometimes one minute can be too long. (3)The human mind was God's idea. Suppose He has goals and ideas designed to bring out the best in us—if the brain is not clogged. (4) Focus! When our mind is focused and we begin to achieve the success-oriented plans God has for us, then we are free to make sacrifices and begin to help others attain their God-planned goals.

> *"The problem is that man has not learned how to tie together success and the Scriptures."*

Does the Bible Speak to Our Desire to Succeed?

Take a moment and study the notions thrown at the one who wants to set some goals and aspire to new heights. As you review the questions posed on pages 4 and 5, stop and ask—Is it possible those questions are mainly all about the same thing? What is the one big need? To tie together success and the Scriptures? Does the Bible speak to that desire, to that need?

In fact, the Bible is remarkably full of "success ideas." And the Bible does speak to our desire to succeed. Then what's the problem?

The problem is that man has not learned how to tie together success and the Scriptures. Or if he has learned how, he often forgets how to reconcile success ideas with spiritual ideas. There have been hundreds of books written that deal with the spiritual side of life, and thousands written to give ideas about greatness, but very few attempt to tie the two together and wrestle with those questions.

The Centipede/Frustration Complex

Are you acquainted with that little crawling worm-like creature called a "centipede?" If you're not, enjoy Webster's Dictionary definition—*"any of a class (Chilopoda) of long flattened many segmented predaceous arthropods with each segment bearing one pair of legs of which the foremost pair is modified into poisonous fangs."* The centipede seems to have legs everywhere. I read a poem that went like this:

> *"The centipede was quite happy,*
> *Until a frog in fun*
> *Said, 'Pray, which leg goes after which?'*
> *That worked her mind to such a pitch,*
> *She lay distracted in a ditch*
> *Considering how to run."* [2]

We have it better than that centipede. Let's enjoy what we have. But what about the person who only hears of ideas from his friends or his favorite success book, but he never reads the Bible to see what it has to say about success? That person may develop a frustration complex. Let's consider how to get out of the centipede/distraction ditch.

Exciting Concepts to Consider While in the Chase

Believe that God has something better for us than the centipede complex. Take a look at what I choose to call...

Six Exciting Concepts:

1. God should know more about success than anyone who has ever written on the subject.
2. God put men and women into the world to succeed, not fail.
3. God is interested in your being successful, provided your definition of success is right.
4. God is interested in goals—in helping you formulate some that would benefit you tremendously.

5. God has written a Book and shared within its pages some excellent principles of success.
6. God knows more about how to motivate you than any other authority in the field. Once He helps you in the formulation of your goals, He then provides inner motivation for maximum achievement.

Like the opening story of this chapter about Nate, there's nothing that's fun or exciting about dividing your life into segments. Don't try that "weekday, work-a-day, here's where I get ahead" personality. Don't split off into the type of thinking that says, "I don't have time to worship on the first day of the week. I have better things to do that will help me a lot more than to meet with others and honor God." You need to feed that incredible brain some success thinking, like—"Hey brain, we're not dividing this mind up into segments any more. If God has time for me every day, I'll have time for Him every day—just like He asked me to."

Speaking of segmenting, have you heard about the farmer who had a good friend who was a car salesman? One day the salesman told him he was considering moving out of the city, getting a house with some acreage and buying a cow. When the car salesman came out to the farm sometime later to talk, the farmer was geared up and ready. The expected question came, "What are you asking for this cow?" The farmer reached in his back pocket and pulled out the folded paper with all the information. "Basic cow, $800; two-tone extra, $180; extra stomach, $300; produce storage compartment, $240; dispensing device-four spigots at $40 each, $160; genuine cowhide upholstery, $500; dual horns, $60; automatic fly swatter, $140. TOTAL PRICE—$2380."

Not everything needs to be segmented! The Bible says, "Any kingdom divided against itself will be ruined, and a house divided against itself will fall."[3] Let's make sure the success parts and the spiritual parts of the *kingdom of our brain* aren't divided!

Review that list of "Exciting Concepts to Consider." With those six concepts fresh in your mind, why not feed it further with three good Proverbs. "A joyful heart makes a face cheerful[4]...a cheerful look brings joy to the heart[5]...and a cheerful heart has a continual feast."[6] After we refresh our minds with those Six Exciting Concepts, we can tell our heart to tell our brain to *tell* our face to cheer up!

Who knows? That brain may begin to defrost! Then we'll be ready to feed some important ideas into the brain again.

2

YOUR SUCCESS DRIVE:
WHERE DOES IT COME FROM?

> *Don't give up on God! One entire generation did, nearly all of those who surrounded Moses! They would not believe that the God of Moses could provide enough power to help them attain their long range hoped-for goals. So God went to a younger generation. God gave Joshua some important pre-requisites. Never forget, pre-requisites nearly always precede a great promise. God used two very special words in that promise, two words He pulled out of His vocabulary,* **"For then you will make your way prosperous, and then you will have good success!"**[1]
>
> **—God to the younger Joshua**

Have you seen the new Father's Day card? It started off great—the front cover said it loud and clear.

"*Dad, I feel like I've inherited a lot of your qualities,*
and I just wanted to let you know . . .

The inside of the card is all blank, except for one line near the top . . .

"*I don't hold it against you.*"

With only that one line inside, there's plenty of blank space for the son or daughter to write an opinion. Who knows what they will write. No doubt they may write in some great traits they think they have inherited!

The Chase

*   *   *

Two older men were discussing hearing aids. One asked, "Did you get that hearing aid yet? You said you were thinking about one of those new tiny ones that can't be seen by most people. "Did you buy it? Do you like it? Are your kids glad?" The other man replied, "They don't know I have it. It's fun just listening. I've already changed my will three times."

*   *   *

Inheritance! What comes to your mind when you mention that word? Some people think of a monetary inheritance from a relative. Medical research professionals and doctors may think of genetics when they speak of an inheritance. Tall kids who think they have inherited some size, and maybe some athleticism, may dream of a basketball career. And all of us would like to think or hope we've inherited some sharp qualities in the mind.

> *"Almost everyone possesses an inner urge, an inner desire or an inner craving to achieve, to accomplish."*

What Is Our Inheritance?

Adam and Eve—what did they inherit? What did they already possess as an inheritance once they were created and placed in the world? Was there something there that motivated them? Was there enough power to keep them motivated from the beginning? What was it?

Joshua—what did he inherit? A huge job! He inherited the job of trying to fill the shoes of Moses. Moses, with God's hand upon him, seemed to have shoes too big for any person to fill,

You, and me—those of us alive today, what did I inherit? What did you inherit? What would you guess?

For years, biblical scholars have placed a big emphasis on Adam, on what we have inherited from him. Don't negate that. We have all been affected negatively by Adam's choice.

But think from the other side. What have we humans inherited— from God? In the next chapter we will look deeper into what some experts have said about our inheritance.

Major on one thought for now. Almost everyone possesses an inner urge, an inner desire or an inner craving to achieve, to accomplish. If you agree with that, then the following question is not necessary. But someone could still ask, *"Is it all right to want to be successful?"*

Success? What is success? Can you define success? One dictionary defines success as "the satisfactory accomplishment of a goal sought for." And at this point, we will only mention that dictionary definition. Is there a name we could attach to that inner urge, that inner desire that you and I have, a desire to seek to accomplish things, to accomplish goals? Why not call it—*a success drive!*

The Brain's Need for Success

Most of us just know we would like to be successful. One writer suggests that you don't just want to be successful, you need to be successful. Your system demands it. Dr. William Burnham, writing about the normal mind, titled one of his chapters, "Success As A Stimulus." He says: "The need of success as a wholesome stimulus is universal. Children have an enormous appetite for it. They need large doses. Adults become depressed without it. It is vital for the normal. The diseased are often cured by it. The modern method in the best hospitals of giving the patient as far as possible interesting work, something worthwhile to do, has demonstrated its value for health. It is the gravest error for physicians, social workers, and teachers not to employ this stimulus."[2]

Inheritance? Sounds like we inherited something very important—

from the mind of God. Achievement and accomplishment are built-in desires. There is a dream of success in the human brain. Man can be analyzed or admonished, and sometimes nothing happens. He can experience approval, appreciation, and praise, and some may even then not get very excited. But when a person feels deep within that he has achieved and accomplished something, the personality comes alive, and a sense of excitement rises and points upward.

For example, watch a small child from the time the child begins to play in the crib. The child is interested in one thing—"satisfactory accomplishment of a goal sought for." The child craves success, exactly as the dictionary defines it. The child will appear unhappy if the goal is not accomplished. The child is doing nothing wrong, just following an inbred desire, doing what comes naturally, doing what his brain is designed to do, according to Dr. Burnham.

Motivated or not-motivated, we need to watch for the sinkers.

Downers, Sinkers and Roadblocks—Danger Points

Built-in desires serve a dramatic purpose. But along the way, danger points appear. The danger points could be given several names—downers, or sinkers, or roadblocks. Any of the three terms could be appropriate to describe what can happen to motivation.

Downers come in different forms. According to Webster's Dictionary, a downer can be (1) a depressing drug; (2) a depressing experience or situation.

In the 21st century, we have learned far more than we want to know about downers. Prison populations have exploded due to illegal drugs that have affected the minds, or the crimes that have been committed to steal those drugs.

But not all downers are illegal drugs. Look at the second part of the definition of downer—"a downer can be a depressing experience or situation." Depressing situations can then lead to depressed lives and depressed minds. Downers are everywhere and can appear anywhere at any time in the mind!

A sinker is another word that could be used to describe those downers. Motivated or not-motivated, we need to watch for the sinkers. Anyone who has fished with a cane pole, a line, a cork, and a hook, knows what a sinker does. It sinks the hook and the bait for the fish to see. Then the cork lets you know if a fish is biting the bait. Sinkers are good to help you catch fish, but sinkers or downers in life can destroy built-in motivation. Sinkers in life are no fun.

Roadblocks could also be another term to describe what goes on around us. Wrong thoughts seem to enter any mind that desires to achieve or aim for success. The first temptation that ever came to Adam and Eve came through an outsider, working on their minds Even today, temptations constantly seek to enter our minds.

These mental roadblocks are everywhere, and there is no way to list them all. But here are some starters. Remember, any mental roadblock could possibly be aimed at defeating your success drive.

Mental Roadblock # 1 –"These are the toughest times ever!"

Just feeding a statement into the mind can sink the spirit. The truth is that these are tough times. But tough times must never be used as an excuse for lethargy. Question: Are these the toughest times? Other generations did not possess half the opportunities we have. Some have estimated that 90 percent of the entire world's knowledge since the days of Adam and Eve has been gained in the past few years. Whatever the statistic, the increase in knowledge while we have been alive has been astounding. These are times of challenge, but times of challenge can motivate us to do better things.

Tough times can be a good time to consider, "What am I doing here? Why is it that I'm alive now, instead of having lived centuries ago?"

The Chase

The alternatives are only two. Either God blundered or He knew exactly what He was doing in allowing you to live in today's world. If He did not blunder, then God has matched you with this generation. He must have seen the potential of accomplishing through each of us exactly what needed to be accomplished in today's world. Or, did He make a mistake in not preserving some of the giants of the past to be alive now? No! You can ask Him why, but the truth is—He chose us—you and me—to face whatever tough times come our way. Knowing God makes no mistakes, maybe our lives should be wonderfully alive with the challenge of adventure.

Mental Roadblock # 2 -"My motivation must be stuck. I can't seem to get motivated."

A goal-oriented person has a real problem at this point, mainly when he or she seeks motivation in the wrong place or the wrong source. The individual who must always be motivated from without is in trouble. When the boss is around to push him hard, he becomes an achiever. But what about when the boss is not around. . . . ?

When a raise in the paycheck is "big enough" or the order given by the supervisor is "loud enough," the worker moves. In some cases, action comes only when he is assaulted by fear. Of course, the best motivation comes from within. And who, do you suppose, knows the most about that?

Mental Roadblock # 3 - "I'm happy just like I am."

Is happiness the biggest goal you want for your life? It is possible to turn inward so much that we forget everyone around us.

Mental Roadblock # 4 - "Okay, I would like to achieve more, but I'm not sure that's what God wants me to do."

This could be the biggest obstacle yet. After all, who needs to accomplish anything as long as he or she can blame God for his personal non-accomplishment? The person who decides "I am just like God made me" may be seeking to blame God for what could possibly just be laziness. In the parable of the talents, the Bible has harsh words for those who fail to achieve more than just what the Master gave him to begin with. That parable emphasizes you should take what you have been given from the start, and make it your purpose to cause it to greatly increase in value. Then you can hear the words, "Well done!"

Excuses do not help us. I may say to myself, "There are many things more important than success." Or, "I haven't achieved much, but I have a great family." Or, "I just consider it more important to be something than to have something." But those are sinkers to the achievement drive God placed in the human mind. I must never be content being anything less than what God intended me to be!

God Has More

Allow me to use an old, old illustration that makes a point. Years ago, browsing in my college library, I came upon an antiquated book with a unique title, "Service." I scanned the book for a few minutes, and hit on one illustration that stuck with me. The prices were out of date when I saw the book, but the point is very important. It went something like this . . .

"Metal scrap iron in a junk yard is worth only pennies per pound. But made into a steam engine for a train, it is worth 25 cents per pound; made into scissors or razors, it's $25 per pound; made into medical instruments, it's $100 per pound. But if that metal is made into tiny parts for watches, it may be worth $500 per pound."[3]

I find it incredible for a man or woman to think that God would want to leave them alone, leave them to settle into a state of mediocrity, and never attempt to reshape them. The point, regardless of the obsolete prices, is a point that needs to stick in our minds. We desperately need to see how much more valuable our lives can become.

Who Gets to Decide What's Valuable?

I have just finished suggesting that God has more to offer than just to put His success-drive in the human mind. But the question still comes to some, "Does He?"

What makes our lives valuable? In our day, we've seen the bold suicide-minded terrorists who are willing to sacrifice their lives for what they believe. Aren't we also faced with bold atheists who are seeking to destroy the spiritual roots of believers in God? There are also a growing number in classrooms who seek to feed ideas into the minds of students, ideas with the potential of destroying motivation and harming the success-drive of those students.

Suppose your college professor handed you a syllabus for you to master these six basic ideas during the semester:

Class Goal # 1—There is no absolute truth.
Class Goal # 2—There is no absolute standard of right and wrong.
Class Goal # 3—There are no absolutes—period. Everything is relative.
Class Goal # 4—Every person's ideas are to be respected.
Class Goal # 5—Your friend's idea on a subject may be as good or better than yours, so be tolerant.
Class Goal # 6—There is no set standard to decide what is good and what is evil.

Would you want to attend that university? Would you be anxious to use your high grade-point average earned in high school to win a scholarship to that university?

Would you desire to take out a student loan to attend that school, where the tuition rate has just gone up another 5 percent?

Does the professor or the university get to decide what's valuable for you?

Do you want a world where there are no standards?

> **Man was so designed that the main way failure could enter one's life would be to chase a plan other than the plan of God.**

Watch What You Chase

There is an important axiom in life, often forgotten. *You may find whatever you are looking for.* Or God may intervene. So you need to watch the ideas you chase, and watch the ideas that chase you. But you are the one who makes the decisions as to what you will chase.

As you continue into Chapter 3: "Success Image; Failure Image?" you'll discover the importance of the decisions you make and how they impact life. Man was so designed that the main way failure could enter one's life would be to chase a plan other than the plan of God. Success and motivation are not man's doing, but God's! What we chase is our choice.

3

SUCCESS IMAGE; FAILURE IMAGE?

Someone asked George Beverly Shea how much he knew about God. He said, "Not much, but what I do know has changed my life."
—*Billy Graham*

Are we to believe that the same God who engineered a successful creation, gave man a successful human body, assigned man tasks which demanded success is also the same God that would stamp man's brain with a failure image?
—*whc*

Dr. Maxwell Maltz, a brilliant plastic surgeon, wrote a bestselling book, *Psycho-Cybernetics,* because he could not escape sharing some observations he made after he removed scars from his patients.

His description? "Some patients show no change in personality after surgery. In most cases a person who had a conspicuously ugly face, or some 'freakish' feature corrected by surgery, experiences an almost immediate (usually within 21 days) rise in self-esteem, self-confidence. But in some cases, the patient continued to feel inadequate and experienced feelings of inferiority. In short, these 'failures' continued to feel, act and behave just as if they still have an ugly face."[1]

After studying patients over a period of time, Dr. Maltz concluded that some have success "instincts." Others feel doomed to failure—possess failure instincts—and consequently, these patients invariably fail.

The Chase

> *If you stare into the mirror each morning, never having meaningful goals for the day, you may have become a victim of a mediocrity image which could lead to a failure image.*

I'm not sure anyone would admit to wanting or having or possessing a failure instinct. However, some seem to easily drift, day by day, into mediocrity. A mentality of mediocrity can make for a slippery slope. If Dr. Maltz is right in his conclusion at this point (we shall analyze other concepts of his later), you either have a success image or a failure image. You are definitely not a Mr. or Ms. In-Between.

Let's tell it like it is. If you stare into the mirror each morning, never having meaningful goals for the day, you may have become a victim of a mediocrity image which could lead to a failure image. You may rise in indignation to protest that you are a Bible-believing Christian, but the truth still stands—you may have a failure image. You may be expecting nothing meaningful from the day, envisioning no great accomplishments, and we usually get exactly what we expect.

Success and Creation

It might help each of us, here at the outset, to just admit that God's first choice each day is not to go around handing out failure-images. What God does is never mediocre. Take a look back—way back in time. His main interest? His goal for the human race? Take a guess.

There is a wonderful excitement even in the oft-heard story of creation. The first chapter of Genesis exclaims: "And God saw the light, that it was good"[2]—KJV "And God called the dry land earth, and the gathering of the waters He called seas; and God saw that it was good."[3] Later God commanded the grass to grow and the trees to yield fruit, ". . . and God saw that it was good."[4] When the sun and moon were thrust into the sky by God Himself, ". . . and God saw that it was good."[5]

Creative activity continued with the cattle of the field and the beasts of the earth and "God saw that it was good."[6]

Some excellent comments about God's success in creation are shared in a little booklet by Dr. Walter Wilson titled, "Wonders of Nature."

An unbeliever once said, "I will believe only what I can understand; none of that mystery stuff for me." He was asked to explain this problem: How is it possible for a black cow to eat green grass which makes white milk and churns yellow butter?

Can you explain this mystery of God? Note some other mysteries of His creation. Consider the remarkable transformation that takes place when a caterpillar (an upholstered worm) encases itself in its homemade casket and is changed into a beautiful butterfly. Its hair is changed to scales—a million to the square inch; the many legs of the caterpillar become the six legs of the butterfly; the yellow becomes a beautiful red; the crawling instinct becomes a flying instinct.

Thus will God take the life of a sinner and transform it until it glows with the beauty of the Lord and is fragrant with the graces of Heaven.

A handful of sand is deposited by the Lord in the heart of the earth. Great heat is applied from beneath and ponderous weight from above until, when it is found by man, it has been miraculously changed into a beautiful, fiery opal.

God takes a handful of black carbon, plants it deep in the bowels of the earth, treats it with heat below, presses it with rocks of the mountains above, and transforms it into a glorious diamond fit for a king's crown.

As God performs these wonderful miracles in nature, He also can transform the souls of men and renew their hearts if they only trust fully in Christ Jesus, the Lord of life.

God knows how to regulate nature. Only the One who made you can successfully direct you. Only the One who made your brain and your heart can successfully guide them to a profitable end.

God's wisdom is seen in the structure of the elephant. The four legs of this great beast bend forward in the same direction. No other quadruped is so made. God planned that this animal should have a huge body, too large to live on two legs. For this reason He gave it four fulcrums so that it could rise from the ground easily.

God's wisdom is revealed in His arrangements of sections and segments as well as in the number of grains.

- *Each watermelon has an even number of stripes on the rind.*
- *Each orange has an even number of segments.*
- *Each stalk of wheat has an even number of grains.*

Another mystery as yet unsolved by man is this: God causes the limb of a tree to grow straight out from the trunk for a distance of forty, fifty, or sixty feet, with no other anchorage than fifteen or eighteen inches of fibers which lose themselves in the trunk of the tree. No human being has discovered how to apply this principle in the construction of buildings or bridges.

God takes oxygen and hydrogen, both of them odorless, tasteless, and colorless, and combines them with carbon which is insoluble, black and tasteless. The result of this combination is beautiful, white, sweet sugar. How does God do it? I do not understand.

I know only that God can take your life—drab, useless and fruitless— and transform it into a beautiful garden of the sweetest graces for His glory. He will do this for you, if you will trust your life to Him![7]

Success and the First Man

The same God who pioneered success with the first five days of created activity personalized success on the sixth day.

He thrust into a shell of skin some 263 bones, and wrapped them in 500 muscles. He perfected a little heart six inches in length, and only four inches in diameter that would beat

    70 times a minute

        4,200 times an hour

            100,800 times a day

                36,792,000 times a year

                    and 2,575,440,000 times in 70 years.

So successful was the little heart that every time it would beat it would pump blood at the rate of

    2½ ounces per beat

        175 ounces per minute

            656 pounds an hour

                and 7 and 3/4 tons in one day.

Small wonder that the psalmist would rejoice and say, "I will praise Thee, for I am fearfully and wonderfully made."[8]

> *Though the end result of achievement is different with different individuals, no man or woman should be content to be less than God's best.*

Success and "God's Image"

For man to be content to be mediocre is not pleasing to God. Though the end result of achievement is different with different individuals, no man or woman should be content to be less than God's best. Success is not measured by what we are. It is measured by what we are compared to what we could be.

At the outset, the first man Adam was all he could be. Before sin entered, he was totally in the image of God. What does that mean? Dr. Walter Thomas Conner is enlightening at this point.

"We are told in Genesis 1:26, 27 that God made man in His own image and likeness. What does this expression mean? . . . in what respects is man like God? . . . what are some of the essential functions or powers that belong to man as a spiritual personality?"[9]

Then Dr. Conner answers his own question:

(1) The first that should be mentioned is intelligence or the power to think—the lower animals possess this power in a very crude and elementary sense. Man has the power to know. . . .

(2) The second thing is the power of rational affection—the lower animals have sensibility and instinctive affection. But man rises above the lower animals as much in his life of sensibility and affection as he does in his thought life. Rational love is the highest moral quality in God and in man. . . .

(3) The third thing is free will—Man is a free being. He has the power of self-determination. He can be influenced but not forced. In this respect he is like God. God is the only perfectly free being in the universe . . . . Man's freedom is limited but real. He has the power to form ideals and then to direct his energies toward the attainment of those ideals. . . .

(4) Another respect in which man is like God is in the possession of the moral sense—in the general use of the term that is what is meant by conscience. Man has the innate sense of right and wrong."[10]

Note that every one of the four aspects of personality is a success necessity designed to point man in an upward direction.

But there is another side to the "Image of God." A. H. Strong suggests, "In what did the image of God consist? We reply that it consisted in (1) Natural likeness to God, or personality; (2) Moral likeness to God, or holiness."[11] Have you ever summarized the first man with the mathematical process of addition?

4 success necessities (listed above)

+

1 moral likeness to God
SUCCESS

Man was so designed that the only way failure could gain entrance to his life was for him to consider some plan other than the plan of God and some other will other than the will of God.

God preceded man with success, challenged man by success, prepared man for success, and then presented man in His own image. Success was not man's doing, but God's!

This might be an excellent place for a multiple choice test question. In your mind's eye, circle either the (a) or (b).

Question—God expected Adam to have
(a) A success image?
(b) A failure image?

THE BIBLICAL BEGINNING OF FAILURE IMAGE

C.S. Lewis, in The Screwtape Letters, vividly describes Satan's strategy: He gets Christians to become preoccupied with their failures; from then on, the battle is won.

—Erwin Lutzer, The Back Door to Success

Of course God wants us to succeed in the task He has given us. He wants us to be mightily motivated, full of confidence, excited about life.

—whc

Now let's talk about defects. How about a moment of honest appraisal?

"On their honeymoon, the groom took his bride by the hand and said, 'Now that we're married, dear, I hope you won't mind if I mention a few little defects that I've noticed about you.' 'Not at all,' the bride replied with a deceptive sweetness. 'It was those little defects that kept me from getting a better husband.'"

Those little defects—those irritating little defects—are a very real part of each of us. We try to laugh it off by emphasizing our good aspects. For instance, if I'm certain God is interested in the total me (Chapter 1), if I'm thoroughly convinced I could be more successful than I am (Chapter 2), and if I have no problem believing God stamped the first man with a success-image (Chapter 3), then it's easy to brag on myself, "I don't have any hang-ups at all!" But what about those few little defects?

On close examination it is evident that something has happened to the successful person God created. For instance, each of us could ask:

The Chase

"Where do I get my negative ideas about success? Why do I always have to be pushed? Sometimes it seems I have no motivation at all. How is it that I can feel so successful one day and so like a failure the next? Why is it that so many things about my life are not pleasing to God?"

Tough questions—real tough. And the questions are not made any easier by the discussion about man in the image of God. If I'm in God's image, shouldn't I be an outstanding success? Shouldn't I have a success image like the first man? Then why the blue-collar blues or the white-collar blahs?

Adam and Modern Man

Who said you were in God's image? That was Adam, remember?

The mistaken idea that each of us is automatically made in God's image could have come from several sources. Perhaps when the minister's sermon mentioned God's image, the mind believed what it wanted to believe and an inner voice said, "That's me!" Or occasionally the idea has been advanced by a success author, usually the one who ignored God through the first two thirds of His book.

At any rate, the idea that modern secular man is in the image of God is only half right. In the last chapter we learned that the image of God consisted of both a natural likeness and a moral likeness.

Every man has a good batting average, because every man has a natural likeness to God (personality). He still has intelligence, or the power to think; power of rational affection; power to form ideals and direct energies toward attainment; and an innate sense of right and wrong.

But there is still something missing. Since man was created not only with that natural likeness but also a moral likeness to God, we suddenly discover the cause of our defects.

We can possess all aspects of the natural likeness, but if there is no moral likeness we cannot truthfully say we are in God's image. And when we are honest, we admit that in the moral area (holiness), someone has been tampering with us. We have computer trouble. Consequently, it is not unusual for some of us to possess either an outright failure-image or a not-much-better mediocrity image.

How the Success Image Got Tarnished

According to the Bible, there are two supernatural powers, each thoroughly capable of brain programming.

Programmer "A" always thrusts in excitement and thrill and purpose. This is the one who challenged man by success, created man in success, appointed man over success and prepared man for success. Adam, after receiving that kind of input, thought, "Great!"

Not very far down the road of success Adam met **Programmer "B."** Now remember that up to this point Adam was programmed right and motivated right. As long as he would stick with God he was bound for success. He would achieve everything God intended for him to achieve, meet every goal in God's plan for his life, and enjoy life to the hilt.

Programmer "B" suggested he had a better mousetrap! "I can give you new insights, new knowledge—just come my way," Satan suggested. So Adam received new knowledge (wrong kind), new insights (became sin-oriented) and to top it all lost the one thing which had made him supremely happy. His fellowship with God was suddenly nil. **Programmer "B"** (Satan) had filled Adam's mind with wrong information and computer foul-up resulted.

From then until now, man has had difficulty in both success and motivation. While desiring to be continually motivated toward success, he knows there are weaknesses within.

Before God can move in and correct the weaknesses, it might be necessary for us to examine some of our basic concepts which influence our entire philosophy of success.

PART TWO:

A Time for Tough Questions

5

HOW MUCH MONEY SHOULD A CHRISTIAN MAKE?

Make all you can,
save all you can,
give all you can.
—*John Wesley*

Money has never made a man happy yet, nor will it. There is nothing in its nature to produce happiness. The more a man has, the more he wants. Instead of its filling a vacuum, it makes one. If it satisfies one want, it doubles and triples that want another way. That was a true proverb of the wise man, rely upon it: "Better is little with the fear of the Lord, than great treasure, and trouble therewith."
—*Benjamin Franklin*

Jesus told a story about a rich man and the man's main emphasis was on MY crops, MY barns, MY grain, and MY goods. God stepped in to assure him he had less than twenty-four hours to live, and commented, "You fool!"[1]

The money question and the selfishness that generally goes with it has ruined many a person along the route to success. Other major questions are involved (questions about success books, proper success definitions, and the question of how to feel successful). But the question more people think about is the money question. How does money relate to success? Does it relate at all? Is money the root of all evil? Is it just a necessary evil? Is it evil at all? What should be the relation of a Christian to money-making?

> *"There is only one type of life for a Christian to live—and the making of money through honest work is a vital part of it."*

A Christian Should Make Money

The Bible definitely teaches that money-making is to be a part of the life of a follower of God. Recently one of the nation's newsmagazines talked about a fad to not believe in work. That's not hard to figure. Some younger people, noting how the older generation has worshiped money, have gone to the opposite extreme. But we must not ignore the Bible command, "Six days you shall labor."[2] There's nothing new under the sun! Ancient Thessalonica is an excellent example to prove that our twenty-first-century thinking is 20 centuries out of date.

Thessalonica had some Christians who believed that Jesus would come soon. They formed a "Let's-Just-Wait-for-the-Second Coming" group. And they would not work! They wanted to sit on the highest mountain and watch for the return of Christ. They wouldn't even earn enough money to feed themselves. The Thessalonica Welfare Department could take care of that!

Through Paul, God thundered His commandment, "Work with your hands, just as we commanded you; so that you may behave properly toward outsiders and not be in any need."[3] *The New Living Translation* reads, "Make it your goal to live a quiet life, minding your own business and working with your hands, just as we instructed you before. Then people who are not Christians will respect the way you live, and you will not need to depend on others."

Paul's letter fell on deaf ears to some in the church. So when Paul wrote a second letter to them, he made it even stronger.
"Even while we were with you, we gave you this command: 'Those unwilling to work will not get to eat.' Yet we hear that some of you are living idle lives, refusing to work and meddling in other people's

business. We command such people and urge them in the name of the Lord Jesus Christ to settle down and work to earn their own living."[4]

There is only one type of life for a Christian to live—and the making of money through honest work is a vital part of it.

But How Much?

A question most of us have thought about but few of us have dared to ask is, "How much money should a Christian make?" Can I expect God's favor if I make a lot of money?

Dr. B. H. Carroll, in An *Interpretation of the English Bible*, is stimulating at this point. He asks, "Just how rich does the New Testament allow a Christian to become? Or, what is the New Testament's limit to the amount of wealth a Christian may lawfully acquire?"[5]

"In my early pastorate at Waco I put this very question to my Sunday school, to be answered the following week. There chanced to be present a millionaire from Newark, New Jersey, who had made his money in Texas, Morgan L. Smith. He approached me when the school was dismissed saying that the question interested him personally, and he would leave before the following Sunday, so he would take it as a favor if I would give him the answer in advance.

I read to him this passage from 3 John: "Beloved, I pray that in all things you may prosper and be in health, just as your soul prospers," which I thus interpreted: John would not pray for unlawful things. He did pray that Gaius might prosper financially just as far as was consistent with his prosperity of soul. Therefore, it was lawful to acquire a million, ten million, any number of millions, if the acquisition did no harm to the soul.

But in many cases wealth as gained or as used starved

and sickened the soul. To them any amount was unlawful that worked such result. It was good for such men that God kept them poor; if He allowed to them an increase of wealth at the expense of the soul, it was in anger and as a judgment. Prosperity makes fools of many. The same law applied to health. Some could be well all the time and the soul the better for it. Others, like Jeshurun, kicked when they waxed fat. Many may echo the Bible statement, "Before I was afflicted I went astray."[6]

God is apparently not interested in helping anyone run off and leave his spirituality. If the financial goal-setter wants God on his or her side, let them be certain this facet of their life is under the complete control of Jesus Christ.

Ways Money Ruins

Our materialistic orientation has never wanted to let us consider the fact that money can ruin. And some of us have never considered it because we've never had enough to have to think about it! There are at least five ways, however, in which money can ruin.

1. *Too much money can ruin one's goals.*—Worthy goals become lost. Goals of service and goals of sacrifice fall by the wayside. The one consuming passion—"I must figure ways to make more money."

2. *Too much money can ruin one's family.*—In this case, the individual can stand it, but his kids cannot. Either in teenage years, or at twenty-one, the money Dad provided ruins them.

3. *Climbing the money ladder can destroy character and morals.* The person who is a "climber" may be so anxious to climb and "have it made" that the people they used and manipulated in

their climb can't stand to be around them now. With another person, character may succumb to outright evil. Morality disappears due to the influence of the money he or she has. Man will always seek to rename his sin under the guise of a "new morality" (exactly identical to the old immorality in God's sight), but the result is the same. Character is destroyed,

4. *Too much money may thwart God's purpose for one's life.*— Ever dream of building a big house on a high hill? Who hasn't! What's the motive? Escape? Get away from people? Hide from human need? "Woe to him who gets evil gain for his house, to put his nest on high, to be delivered from the hand of calamity! You have devised a shameful thing for your house by cutting off many peoples; so you are sinning against yourself."[7] Seclusion, whether in a monastery or a "home of my dreams"— that which gets you farther and farther from the people who need you— just doesn't seem to be God's perfect will.

5. *Too much money may over-inflate the ego.*— "Look what *I* did. Let me tell you how *I* made it!" Reread the opening paragraph of this chapter. See any similarities?

God Knows Best

One day it dawned on me that God knew better than I just exactly how much money it would take to ruin me. It was incredible that I (or any Christian) would set a monetary goal and not bathe it in prayer. Believing that God is wonderfully interested in me, and my success for His glory, why should I worry about what I don't have? I ought to thank God daily that He has never been interested in helping me attain so much that my life would be ruined by what I had attained. The one who is yielded and usable can always thank God regardless of the amount of money he has. He can set his goals and strive for them, once he is convinced they are God's goals for his life. Regardless of the amount he possesses, let him trust God's judgment.

Maybe God can use you right where you are! Of course He can! God can use highly successful people in each income bracket of society.

For example, take the lower income bracket. Is it possible God has used successful people in that bracket to show others with very little income how they should live? Wouldn't the same be true of the lower-middle income bracket? The middle bracket? The upper-middle? One statement is worth repeating—God can use successful people in all parts of life. And isn't it reasonable to believe God wants some Christian millionaires who are highly successful in life?

A millionaire commented to me, "The most depraved men I know are millionaires." But many of you would join with me and add a good fact, that there are Godly millionaires that are generous with their gifts to God's work and are wonderfully used of God.

If God put all successful people in the upper income bracket, and if God reserved success only for these, then the other 98 percent of the world's population would never know what it meant to be successful.

> *"This life is the only time we have a chance to give money to God."*

A Special One-Time Chance

No one has forever to decide what he will do with the money God permits him to earn. But in the short time you are alive, you have a special opportunity! This life is the only time we have a chance to give money to God. What is your life? The Bible says, "You are just a vapor that appears for a little while and then vanishes away."[8]

From Heaven, you will not be able to give any amount of your money to advance the work God is trying to do to reach the people on earth. Zero! None! If you are going to give money to God's work, you have to make the decision while you are here.

Ron Blue mentions some Bible verses about giving (Proverbs 3:9-10, and Malachi 3:10-12) and adds, "God is serious about giving. He knows—and He promises—that we will be better off for it. Many people interpret this to mean that the more they give, the more they will get. Were this actually true, giving would become the hottest investment on Wall Street."

About rewards, he says, "God's promised rewards are much more significant than financial blessing. Material reward may—and often does follow a faithful giver, yet it must be neither promised nor expected. Instead, expect God to bless you in ways you may never have imagined. Perhaps He will give you good health, favor with your boss, or wisdom in your financial decision making. He may use your gift chiefly to draw you closer to Himself. He may, in fact, choose to bless you with an eternal reward—one that you will never see this side of heaven. Whatever the case, give cheerfully. Your promised reward will surely come."⁹

The Danger of Greed

"Instruct those who are rich in this present world not to be conceited or to fix their hope on the uncertainty of riches, but on God, who richly supplies us with all things to enjoy. Instruct them to do good, to be rich in good works, to be generous and ready to share, storing up for themselves the treasure of a good foundation for the future, so that they may take hold of that which is life indeed." (I Tim. 6:17-19)

The word "balance" is both a key word and a need word each day God leaves us here on earth. The fine line between need and greed is difficult to discern. After giving God at least His tenth, it is wise to ask Him for extra special wisdom to know how much of the rest to keep for

41

our use.

Whether a mighty member of a Board of Directors, or one who puts in 12 hours a day at a low-paying job, it is good to remember—*people are more important than any of your stuff, things, money in the bank or investments.* Investing in people, and investing in offering people a chance to work and become achievers is high on the "important things" list. It is a God-given gift to know how to make money, and a fantastic gift to know how to wisely use it for His purposes while still alive.

Money is not the root of all evil. Of itself, money is neutral. But the Bible says that the love of money (human greed) is the root of all sorts of evil (1 Tim. 6:10). It is impossible to warn too much against the dangers of greed.

Tolstoy has a powerful story of a young Russian who fell heir to his father's small farm. He was no sooner in possession of this land than he began to dream eagerly, of how he could add to it. One morning a stranger, evidently a person of great power and authority, came to him and told him, as they were standing near the old homestead, that he could have, for nothing, all the land he could walk over in one day—but at sundown he must be back at the very place from which he started. Pointing to the grave of this young man's father, the stranger said, "This is the point to which you must return."

The youth looked eagerly over the rich fields in the distance and throwing off his coat and without waiting to say a word to his wife and children, started off across the fields. His first plan was to cover the tract of ground 6 miles square; but when he had walked the six he decided to make it 9, then 12, then 15—which would give him 60 miles before sundown!

By noon he had covered two sides of this square of 30 miles. But eager to get on and compass the whole distance, he did not stop for food. An hour later he saw an old man drinking at a spring, but in his hunger for land he brushed aside the cup which the old man offered and rushed on in his eager quest for possession of land. When he was a few miles from the goal he was worn down with fatigue.

A few hundred yards from the line he saw the sun approaching the horizon and knew that he had but a few minutes left. Hurrying on and ready to faint, he summoned all his energies for one last effort—and managed to stagger across the line just as the sun was sinking. But as he crossed the line he saw a cruel, cynical smile on the face of the stranger who had promised him the land. Just as he crossed the line—the master and possessor, he thought, of 15 square miles of rich land—the youth fell dead upon the ground which he had coveted.

The stranger then said to the servant, "I have offered him all the land he could cover. Now you see what that is: six feet long by two feet wide; and I thought he would like to have the land close to his father's grave, rather than to have it anywhere else." With that the stranger, who was Death, vanished, saying as he did, "I have kept my pledge."

HOW DO SUCCESS BOOKS RELATE TO THE BIBLE?

The best book of success principles ever printed is the Bible.

—whc

Leonard Ravenhill shared a story I have since captioned, "The Parable of the Contented Frog." Some scientists took a frog and dropped him in hot water. The frog hopped out—fast! They dropped him in a second time. Same result. Then they dropped him in a vat of cold water and he relaxed.

What the frog did not know was that the vat of cold water had a fire beneath it. While the frog relaxed the water was heated ever so gradually. The frog sat there, the temperature of the water rose slowly, and before long the frog had been boiled to death.

Isn't that a parable all of us need to hear? We don't know how it is in the frog world, but in our world, it fits to a T. Mediocrity is the fire. Man, represented by the frog, sits and relaxes until his mediocre ways destroy him. Let him stay content without goals and motivations just so long, and one day he will no longer care to move.

A Test and Some Logic

In the twenty-first century, books have been written which might, in a general way, be designated as "success books." In the average bookstore or library, several titles with this topic can be found. Mostly, these are "How To" books that tell how we can be successful.

What should a Christian do in this area of his thinking? Should he run from these books or run to them? What kind of eye of discernment is needed? How do success books in general relate to the Bible? Is there a conflict?

How about a quiz? This one has only one question. If the statement is true, circle the T. If false, circle the F.

T   F   1. Truth cannot conflict with truth.

That question is not as easy as it looks, is it? But you guessed right if you circled the T. There is just no way truth from one source can conflict with truth from another one. When there is conflict, only one of the ideas is 100 percent true. Deciding which ideas are totally true is not always an easy decision, but truth is truth, and two truths should not conflict.

Let's approach this concept from another direction. This time let's use logic.

1. Truth cannot conflict with truth.
2. Truth in one area cannot conflict with truth in another area.
3. Truth in one area should therefore complement truth in another area.

To word it another way . . .
1. Truth cannot conflict with truth.
2. Truth in the area of success principles cannot conflict with truth in the Bible.
3. Truth in the area of success principles should therefore complement truth in the Bible (and vice versa).

Whatever real truth there may be in a success book, and whatever real truth there may be in the Bible (I believe it to be completely true), logic suggests there should definitely not be a conflict. Review the seemingly conflicting thoughts that we often wrestle with (chap.1, lower half of page 4). If all those questions could be answered correctly, a success book and the Bible could wonderfully complement each other.

Credit Where Credit Is Due

Many Christians are indebted to success books. Permit a word of personal testimony. This book would never have been written had it not been for some "How-To-Do-It" books I stumbled upon a few years ago. What are some of the ways I am indebted to success books? Here are a few of the benefits I gained from success books. They gave me:

1. A good case of dissatisfaction with myself.
2. A good case of hunger for achievement.
3. An opportunity to apologize to the Lord.
   I realized that people in the secular world were willing to pay the price of dedication and achievement that I would not pay— in spite of being in the biggest business in the world.
4. An incredible desire to know how all of the research about success related to God's Word.
5. A great self-image, which incidentally, soon flopped.

And that was, frankly, the best thing that ever happened to me. Because my personally instilled and constantly motivated self-image did not work all the time, I suspicioned others had met failure in the same way. I began to wonder—do you suppose the Bible has something even better to offer?

Success books made this "contented frog" begin thinking about how to get out of the pond of mediocrity. If you're satisfied with your rut-of-routineness, okay. If you even want to blame your lack of motivation and your lack of goal-setting on the Lord, go ahead. Since most everyone does, it is doubtful one more is going to upset the eternal applecart. But if you are tired of blaming God and would like to do something about it, I can recommend you try a success book or two. At least you won't enjoy sitting in the pond of do-nothingness nearly as much. Some of the illustrations of how men dedicate themselves to a goal bring down severe strokes of judgment upon the heads of routine do-nothing Christians.

Fallacies To Watch For

As with any book, the reader of a success book should pray for the wisdom of discernment as he reads. In some books, certainly not all, the reader may quickly spot some of the fallacies listed below.

1.   A few of the books only introduce God somewhere after page 150, if at all. Others are more generous and mention His name every 75 pages or so. The implication, of course, is that God doesn't have very much to do with success, nor does He know very much about it.

2.   Some of the books deal with only one side of life—the materialistic view. It is possible to have it made materialistically and yet be a total flop in life. The very ones who climb the highest may suddenly see failure staring them in the face. What does one do if his personal empire comes crashing down? Or, the materialistically successful man may just feel miserable in his success! Or, his home may fall apart. Or, his drive to get ahead may give him an ulcer, or a heart attack. Is that success?

3.   Some of the books may suggest that man, regardless of his manner of living, is in God's image, and God is anxious to help him succeed. Remember the discussion in Chapters 3 and 4? The moral likeness to God has been corrupted by sin. It is only the personality side of the image that is still intact.

4.   The source of confidence may differ. The Bible suggests that the believer is to put no confidence in the flesh. He or she is not to seek more self-confidence, but Christ-confidence. Self seems to disappoint all of us sooner or later, and if that's the only basis for confidence, there may be a shattering of the personality.

7

HOW CAN I DEFINE SUCCESS?

Success is much more than a matter of achieving the right things; it is also a matter of being the right person.

—whc

We must have something to hold up for our young, as our parents did for us, and say, "This is success, child. Go after it!"

—Howard Whitman

This posted sign was an attention-getter—with lots of truth in it. No doubt it provided a good laugh for all the ambitious young employees.

"Work hard for eight hours a day and don't worry. Then in time you may become a boss and work eighteen hours a day and have all the worry."

Dreams of rising to the top, dreams of reaching goals, dreams of "being successful"—could provide some interesting stories. If you were a reporter in the busy city, doing "on the street interviews," here are a couple of good questions you might ask, "Quick— in one sentence, How do you define success?" Or, "Tell me what you think. What is a good definition of success?"

A question for the reader—how would you define it? What do you think success is?

I was in a taxi-cab in the city of Philadelphia some years ago. As we approached the Schuylkill River, the cab driver asked if I had ever seen a car-crushing machine. "You're about to see your first one then." He continued, "In a few minutes I am going to show you entire automobile bodies rolling along in assembly line fashion on a giant conveyor belt. They will go into a giant car-crushing machine that costs several million dollars. It takes sixty seconds to grind a car to bits."

When I saw the instant-crusher, I reflected on the fact that the desire for achievement grinds up lives nearly that fast. When the average Joe tries to be successful, he chooses one of two approaches. Either his method of achieving what he calls success grinds him to powder; or, his method of achieving what he calls success grinds to powder the lives of all those around him. Anytime success is a life crusher, there is something drastically wrong with the definition.

The word "success" has become a very popular word. I thought I could go to a book store, find books about success, gather several definitions used by the various authors, and then determine a definition all my own. In the first six books that I picked up, no author even attempted to define it. The trend of writers has improved some, but far too many lives still get crushed in the success machine!

Somewhere, sometime soon, we better change our course. Lives are coming apart. More content has been written about success, but more people may know less about how to achieve it than in any preceding generation.

Allow me to illustrate. An insurance man and I were having lunch together. He was telling me that one of the big areas of his work was selling policies to medical doctors. In the course of the conversation he shared a comment which evoked considerable concern.

"A psychiatrist shared with me that of all the counseling cases he handles, at least one third of them are young people. This is a drastic change from five years ago. But now this is the picture of nearly every day's case load."

Other psychiatrists whom my insurance friend later quizzed all agreed their pattern of cases was no different! After that conversation I began to take note of hospitals where I visited. Invariably I am astounded by the percentage of youth needing help. When I mentioned this at a meeting of ministers, one of the clergymen said he walked onto the psychiatric floor of a large metropolitan hospital and there were so many young people, he thought they were having a youth convention!

We can't stand much more of this kind of success!

The hero of a recent modern novel is in a Paris bar after the Wall Street debacle of 1929. The bartender asks him, "Did you lose a lot in the crash?" He answers, "I lost everything I really wanted in the boom!"

Life Is Tough

Many of us have heard stories of men and women who have risen to special heights in the business world, only to have their lives fall apart.

While attending a large conference with several thousand leaders in a major city some years ago, I heard the speaker share the following story:

> When I returned home following service in the military, five of my closest friends were five of my town's leading business and professional men. I was with them constantly because we drank, and drinking is great for compatible companions. These men all had it made.
>
> One of them was the head of a large plant in my state, just one jump from the top bracket in the home office.
>
> Another was the regional head of a large merchandising establishment.
>
> A third was the top leader of another plant in our state, and it was the largest of its kind in our state.
>
> A fourth had been in our state court system, but then began practicing private law.
>
> The fifth was the president of a bank.
>
> Then the speaker shared some sad news. He stated that, as he

spoke, only one of the five was still living. Three had committed suicide, one died while undergoing treatment, and the fifth had to retire from work with a very serious physical disability while still in the 'very noonday' of his life. Then the speaker said, "Were it not for the grace of God, I shudder to think where I would be today."

Almost everyone who has come up through the ranks and risen to a place of leadership has indeed learned that life is tough, and many times real tough. Someone needs to remind us again—making a living is only the means to a goal, but life itself, a successful life fashioned with the special help of God guiding him day by day, that's the real goal.

What Success Is Not

Definitions are important. Before defining what success is, it may be important to define what success is NOT.

Success is not material satisfaction.
"For what shall it profit a man if he shall gain the whole world, and lose his own soul?"[1]

Success is not selfishness.
When an individual sets goals for himself, he must make certain his goals are not self-centered. There is no quicker way for God to withdraw His blessing.

Success is not life without problems.
"In the world you shall have tribulation."[2]

Success is not ego-mania.
Paul wrote to the Galatians, "For if anyone thinks he is something

when he is nothing, he deceives himself."³ Some Christians have black-listed any thought of success because of mistakenly relating it to egomania.

Success is not self-confidence.

Biblical confidence is to be centered on Someone else. "I can do all things through Him [Christ] who strengthens me."⁴ Jack Hyles has wisely noted, "Many a Christian has withstood the onslaught and attacks of the Devil on all sides only to find himself defeated by self-confidence because of his past victories."

Success is not climbing the organizational ladder by walking roughshod over others.

One man Jesus attempted to heal from his blindness was asked whether he could see. He replied, "I see men as trees walking." Jesus knew then that this man was only half healed (still 50 percent sick), and He touched him again and healed him completely. It's a sick man who sees others as no more than trees.

Success is not pleasing everybody.

Try to please everybody, and no one will like you because of your vacillating. "Woe to you when all men speak well of you."⁵

Success is not being a carbon copy.

In the music school of the world's largest seminary (Southwestern Baptist in Fort Worth), they humorously relate the years when many of the music ministers trained there led music with their three main fingers. That's the way the teacher did it! But—he had lost two of his fingers in an accident! The Christian can rejoice, "God does not expect me to be a carbon-copy of anyone!"

Keith Miller, in *A Second Touch*, excitedly exclaims, "What a relief! I saw that I had always been living a life like a suit two sizes too large, sort of hoping I would grow into it. . . . I had never felt at home in my own skin . . . . But now I was discovering that I could just be me, for Christ's sake."[6]

Getting God in the Definition

As you formulate your definition of success, ask, "Is God in my definition of success?" God is not about to be catalogued out of the success business. Yet many want God to help them "succeed" just so they can quickly phase Him out.

That happens even in the spiritual business. One uses his "spirituality" to get self-pity, another uses it to make himself the center of attention, and another uses it to act half-crazy so everybody will notice what he can do—all in the name of spirituality!

A right definition of success is important from two sides—from the side of having God in it, and from the side of having achievement in it. Defining success without having God in the definition leaves man without the blessing of God upon his life. Yet having God in your life and still not achieving is adding insult to the Infinite.

God knows

> More about success than man does
> More about man's needs than man does
> More about goal-setting than man does
> More about inner confidence than man does
> More about power than man does, and
> More about planning life than man does.

Since God knows all those things and provides the very route to our success, isn't it incredible that we would leave Him out of our plans?

> *"Success involves achieving the maximum that can be achieved with what God has given you.*

What Is Success?

It was a typical Monday morning. I had missed the last 3 or 4 days at the YMCA, and the friend in the weight room quizzed me. "Where have you been?" "Been goofing off" (translation—"not exercising"). "Yeah, been goofin' off. You know where that is?" He laughed, denied knowing anything about that place.

We live in that spot in the world that lies just between "'goofin' off" and "getting with it" and we're always pulled between the two. "Rest" is vital before the race, but the starting gun fires new every morning.

One dictionary calls "success" the "satisfactory accomplishment of a goal sought for." Secular man calls it "the prosperous termination of any enterprise."

Wayne Dehoney has conducted several conferences on "Personal Dynamics." In these he has discussed many aspects of success. He defines success as "the progressive realization of a person's worthwhile predetermined goals." He says they must be progressive—with man always moving toward them and always setting more; they must be worthwhile; and they must be predetermined—involving the setting of short-range goals and long-range goals.

Before centering in on one precise definition, some closely related thoughts might help.

> Success involves being right with God.
> Success involves being able to accept yourself.
> Success involves knowing you're on the winning team.
> Success involves winning daily victories.
> Success involves getting along with others.
> Success involves achieving the maximum that can be
> achieved with what God has given you.

The Chase

To get an accurate definition of success, two things must be considered: (1) the individual (2) the individual's goals.

First of all, success must zero in on the continued achievement of being the person God wants you to be. Secondly, you must continue to work on the established goals God helps you to set. A key word here is continue--your achievement must go on. It is a daily process, an hourly process, and at times a minute-by-minute process. It is achievement—reaching for, and accomplishing what you reach toward. It concerns something inside of you. It relates to goals—something that keeps you stretching to become more of what He would have you to be. It is always related to God. And it is connected with what God wants. With that in mind, neither your personal life nor your goals should miss the mark.

Now ask, Am I being successful? Am I continually being the person God wants me to be? Am I continually achieving the goals God helps me set?

Wise was the man who remarked, "We judge ourselves by what we plan to do. Others judge us by what we have done." We might add, "God also judges us by what we have done, rather than by what we plan to do."

Reviewing—success is the continuing achievement of being the person God wants you to be, and the continuing achievement of established goals God helps you set.

Have a go at it! And continue to have a go at it!

8

HOW IS A CHRISTIAN SUPPOSED TO FEEL?

Doctors, and especially those who treat people suffering from nerves, are realizing more and more that just as you must keep the laws of health if you want a healthy body, so there are certain laws of the spirit you must keep if you want a healthy mind, peace and inward happiness.

—Gordon Powell

Be of good cheer. [1]

—Jesus Christ

"All right," the skeptic asks, "suppose I revise my definition of success so that I include both God and goals? What is that supposed to mean? How would I feel? How is a Christian supposed to feel? If I committed my way totally to the Lord, what would happen? What could I expect? I'm sure not interested in heading down Depression Street. Does the Bible tell how a committed Christian should feel?

Not really. The Bible doesn't say a great deal about feeling. But what some do not realize is that the Bible indirectly shares an abundance of thought as well as notable examples on the subject.

While the manuscript for this book was in the early stages, I sensed a problem in a church member's life, and felt impressed of God to ask him to come by the office for a visit. I began the conversation.

"I've wondered if something is wrong. I believe the commitment you made recently was very genuine. Yet I've been watching as you've listened to the visiting minister. Even though he has given one of the best presentations of the spiritual life I have heard, I've noticed that you

59

no longer smile. I wanted to share something with you and ask if this might be your problem."

Then I placed in his hands the material I am about to share with you. He read only a little ways and looked up excitedly. "That's it! I haven't known how to feel. I didn't know whether I was supposed to smile or frown, be excited or sad."

As he later read how a Christian is supposed to feel and how a Christian can arrive at that point, a wonderful sense of relief enlightened his countenance.

If you haven't known how to feel, don't think you are alone in your frustration. That may just be where most of us are. What do you say we wrestle with it a bit?

Take Your Pick

Our suspicions tell us that our feelings should fall in one of three areas. Read closely, and take your pick!

> 1. That "top-of-the-mountain" feeling: the Christian should feel excited, happy, radiant, thrilled all the time.
> *Advantage:* This is what most everyone wants. Sounds great!
> *Disadvantage:* 90 percent of professing Christians would probably admit failure at staying in this category. Most have tried to feel this way, have wanted to feel this way, have read books on how to feel this way and finally in despair have come to say, "For me it just doesn't work." The positive thinking, success-all-the-time feeling has been tried by most, and despair has resulted.
>
> 2. That "just-average" feeling: the Christian is supposed to feel high some of the time, low the rest of the time, expect to feel both up-and-down, high-and-low, and that is the

Christian life. Someway these are probably going to average out. One of the verses in the spiritual, *Nobody Knows the Trouble I've Seen* says, "Sometimes I'm up, sometimes I'm down, Oh, yes Lord!" These words express this theory best of all.

Advantage: The main advantage is that this sounds just like we would expect life to sound. We felt that way when we were unsaved, and still feel that way since being saved. Most Christians we know seem to feel this way.

Disadvantage: No one is quite content with this. We get tired of being average. There is less advantage to salvation, because we felt this way before we were saved. Does God save a man for the purpose of being in despair half the time?

3. The "Mr. Humility" feeling: Man should be extremely humble. He should be lowly-in-spirit, a "turn-the-other-cheek" fellow who lets others walk on him, and then he is bound to be pleasing Jesus.

Advantage: Some could interpret that Jesus encouraged this idea. At least, Jesus was the most humble man who ever lived. He did speak of "turning the other cheek."

Disadvantage: This is a very difficult way to live. When we do so, we even get proud of our humility. We can lose all confidence and become negative. Besides, how can one so humble ever be motivated to be an achiever? "Why those others climbing up the organization ladder of success will trample me under!" And what about the Bible story when Jesus drove money changers out of the Temple?

Made up your mind as to how a Christian should feel? Good. Now grab a pencil and write your choice of Feeling No. 1, Feeling No. 2, or Feeling No. 3. Now hold it for a moment while we move on.

9

HOW DO FEELINGS RELATE TO FAITH?

I know that when I take time to talk to God and obey the promptings of the Holy Spirit I feel alive and life is joyous and exciting.
—Peter Marshall

Life's frustrations are a mystery or a challenge, depending on whether they are confronted by faith.
—whc

One of my friends has a unique thought-provoking method of making people laugh. He never answers a hallway comment as you'd expect. Ask him, "How're you feeling?" and he replies, "Are you a doctor?"

Bertha Smith was a missionary to China for many years. After retirement, she was a frequent speaker in churches. When in her eighties, she was still going strong, so she decided to write a book, *Go Home and Tell.*

Having seen Miss Bertha on various occasions, I was intrigued when I heard one of the ladies ask, "How do you feel?" Her reply, "I don't know. I haven't felt of myself lately!" She simply refused to live by her feelings. She taught people to live by faith.

A warning: don't use the phrase, "How are you feeling?" around certain people as you pass them in the hallway—unless you have lots of time. Some individuals may snarl the face, wrinkle the brow, and take most of the next hour telling you how they feel!

Feelings are not nearly as important as we have made them out to be. But do they ever control us!

> **WARNING:** *It is impossible to live by your faith and your feelings at the same time. It is either-or.*

Six Truths That Could Change Your Life

Most of us sense a vacancy and a void replacing the vitality we long to have. Pick a group of 100 people and 90 of them would express a desire to feel better. All the vitamins in the world cannot permanently solve the crisis of not feeling good because feelings are not based only on the physical condition.

Do you believe God wants you to have inner excitement, radiance, thrill, and happiness? (Please, none of that mushy, fake kind of happiness that turns people off.) If you believe God wants you to have an inner excitement about life, then the following six truths may be extremely important.

1. God is definitely interested in how you feel.
2. Satan is a master at making you feel bad.
3. If you believe your feelings, you may be choosing to believe Satan.
4. The Christian life is not based on feelings.
5. You should learn the fine art of living by faith.
6. Living by faith will make you feel a thousand times better than you ever felt worrying about how you feel.

Now to explain these six truths. Study carefully the next few paragraphs because failure right at this point is the cause of psychiatrists working overtime.

(1) God is definitely interested in how you feel. Jesus knew the tensions of His last week in Jerusalem were almost too much for His

troubled disciples, and He suggested, "Let not your heart be troubled."[1] When the feelings of Mary and Martha were shattered by Lazarus' death, Jesus wept. When a man felt miserable over his past and repented, Jesus promised him a place in paradise. Again, Jesus took special time to speak words to those who mourn, to the poor in spirit, and to those who felt persecuted for righteousness' sake.

Of course God is interested in how you feel. "Cast all your anxieties [that includes your burdens, your frustrations, your feelings] upon Him, because He cares for you."[2] If He cared about the lilies, the lepers, the diseased, and the woman in adultery, wouldn't He care about how you feel? He is anxious that you "be of good cheer."

(2) Satan is a past master at making you feel bad. The trouble with most of us is that we are as confused about supernatural powers on the matter of feelings as Job's three friends were on the matter of suffering. Job's friends believed all suffering had to come from God, and it was sent as punishment for wrongdoing. They never stopped to consider there might be another supernatural power.

When people get saved, Satan soon finds a way to at least make sure they don't always *feel* saved. He doesn't want them to memorize Romans 10:13, John 5:24, John 1:12, and 1 John 5:12. Satan just sends the darts of depression often enough that the average believer will quit reading his Bible because he feels so bad.

When Christians start getting concerned over other Christians, Satan again uses the tactic of making them *feel* bad. As long as he can keep us feeling bad, he thinks he's found a way that will keep us from getting concerned for others. You better believe if Satan can bring boils to Job he can bring depression to you!

Live by your feelings, and Satan will cackle with glee! He is the deceiver! He can deceive you into feeling bad when you have a thousand reasons to feel good. He is a liar! He can whisper to you about how bad you feel when you know that two seconds ago you felt great. Satan is a past master at making you feel bad.

(3) If you believe your feelings, you may be choosing to believe Satan. For years, in speaking engagements, I have used the little phrase, If you feed your faith, your faith will grow. If you feed your doubts, your doubts will grow. Whichever one you feed will surely grow.

The life of a first-year college student is frequently ruined because Satan thrusts a dart of doubt in his direction. So he or she quits reading their Bible (which feeds their faith), going to church on Sunday (which feeds their faith), memorizing Bible promises (which feeds their faith). Instead, he or she spends countless hours reading the writings of skeptics. Then these students can't understand why their doubts have grown—they've fed their doubts!

Feelings of doubt, feelings of despair, feelings of depression, feelings of guilt over something confessed 20 years ago, feelings of lust, feelings of anger—all are put in our mind by the devil. If possible, he wants to keep us far away from "Feeling No. 1."

(4) The Christian life is not based on feelings. The greatest Christians I have known were exciting people to be around. They had troubles and problems the same as anyone else (God has no exempt status for His people), but theirs didn't seem to matter so much. They were excited, happy, radiant, and thrilled in spite of it.

What's the difference?

They had mastered one secret most of us have not yet discovered. The secret? The Christian life is not based on feelings. The Christian life is based on faith.

Andrew Murray, in an excellent little work for new Christians entitled, *The New Life*, explains,

> Between the life of feeling and the life of faith the Christian

has to choose every day. Happy is he who, once and for all, has made the firm choice and every morning renews the choice not to seek or listen for feeling but only to walk by faith according to the will of God. The faith that keeps itself occupied with the Word, with what God has said and, through the Word, with God Himself and Jesus His Son, shall taste the blessedness of a life in God above. Feeling seeks and aims at itself; faith honors God and shall be honored by Him. Faith pleases God and shall receive from Him the witness in the heart of the believer that he is acceptable to God.[3]

The word "faith" is in the New Testament (NASB version) 246 times. The word "believe" is in the New Testament 136 times. "Faith" and "believe" are from the same Greek word, the only difference being in the noun or verb ending. Yet the word "feel" or "feeling" is only in the New Testament 7 times, 6 of those for "feel" and only 1 for feeling. What is significant is to note that when "feel" or "feeling" is used, it has nothing to do with telling us how to live.

Word usage in the New Testament is a powerful weapon in re-emphasizing the fact that the Christian life is based on faith, and is definitely not based on our feelings. And that is great news!

These New Testament words give additional emphasis to the fact that the Christian life is based on our faith, definitely not our feelings.

(5) You should learn the fine art of living by faith. Mention the word faith and some only think of something that happened twenty years ago when they put their faith in Christ. They must think the only meaning of faith is fire insurance!

Faith is fantastic, everyday excitement. Without it, you're doomed to despair. Viktor Frankl rotted for years in a concentration camp during World War II and later wrote: "The prisoner who had lost faith in the future—his future—was doomed. With his loss of belief in the future, he also lost his spiritual hold; he let himself decline and become subject to mental and physical decay."

WARNING: It is impossible to live by your faith and your feelings at the same time. It is either-or.

As you seek to master the art to live by your faith, review often these words of Andrew Murray. "Therefore let faith always speak against feeling. When feeling says, 'In myself I am sinful, I am dark, I am weak, I am poor, I am sad,' Let faith say, 'In Christ I am holy, I am light, I am strong, I am rich, I am joyful.'"[4]

(6) Living by faith will make you feel a thousand times better and give you the inner happiness you've always wanted. If you've tried years of living by feelings, is it asking too much to live by faith? If living by feelings has not brought happiness, is it really a gamble to try believing God's promises? One verse—memorized—Ephesians 3:20—could start you down the new path.

> *"Thank You that You see all my problems as opportunities for You to work miracles of accomplishment."*

What Does a Christian Do on a Blue Monday?

Relying on faith instead of feeling should not seem strange to the believer. But in case it does, here's one way to get started.

Think back in time and review your conversion experience. But salvation didn't come because of a certain feeling.

Salvation came on the day when, by faith, you opened your heart to admit that you were a sinner and needed a Saviour.

Maybe your prayer went something like this: "Lord, I need you. By faith I open the door of my heart. I now repent of my sin. Forgive my sin. I want you to be my Saviour and Lord. Take control of my life. Make me the kind of person you want me to be." When you prayed that kind of prayer, something happened to change your life, didn't it?

Now, on that blue Monday (by the way, blue Mondays frequently come on Fridays) when your feelings want to drag bottom, I hope you'll get to the end of your rope again. You might pray a new desperation prayer that would sound like this: "Lord, I've been miserable today because I've been living by my feelings. I apologize, Lord. I want to thank You today that You say in Your Word that I am saved, that whosoever would call upon the name of the Lord would be saved. Thank You, Lord, that Your Word means that the day I called upon You, repented of my sin, and turned my heart and life over to Christ, I was saved.

Thank You that You see all my problems as opportunities for You to work miracles of accomplishment. Thank You that You are able to do exceeding abundantly above all I ask or think! Thank You that today is going to be a great day because You are working on my behalf."

The apostle Paul said, "For we walk by faith, not by sight."

Try the faith walk very long, and Feeling No. 1 may be just around the corner. It was for Paul, but you'd never dream of the unorthodox way the apostle arrived there.

PART THREE:

Starting Down the Success – Image Trail

10

PAUL'S BUILT-IN SUCCESS IMAGE

I have no trouble wondering if God wants me to succeed.
The cross is proof enough for me.
—whc

Our feelings are revealed by our actions.
—John Haggai

Every Christian prefers Feeling No. 1. Every Christian wants that mountain-top feeling, the feeling of excitement! Happiness is to be excited!

Is this a wrong desire? Not at all. When God created man, He made him supremely happy. Man was excited from the first moment he was created! Sin was the factor that made him less than God's best. When man gets right with God, he should be supremely happy and excited about life, regardless of circumstances. Paul was.

Right at the Top

Bible scholars consider the apostle Paul the greatest Christian. In his field, Paul became an outstanding success. He was aggressive, motivated, and a positive thinker.

Scholar F. W. Farrar, writing one of the great classics on the life of the apostle, said years ago:

How little did men recognize his greatness! Here was one to whom no single man that has ever lived, before or since, can furnish a perfect parallel. If we look at him only as a writer, how immensely does he surpass in his most casual Epistles, the greatest authors, whether Pagan or Christian, of his own arid succeeding epochs. If we look at the Christian world, the very greatest worker in each realm of Christian services does but present an inferior aspect of one phase only of Paul's many-sided preeminence.[1]

Later Farrar discussed Paul as a theologian, a preacher, a practical organizer, a missionary, and a reformer who altered the course of history, before concluding, "No saint of God has ever attained the same heights in so many capacities."

Rising Above Circumstances

Whatever Paul's plan may have been (and we shall uncover his marvelous secret in later chapters), Paul definitely found a way to arrive at Feeling No. 1. And Paul did not maintain his daily thrill and excitement because of his circumstances but in spite of his circumstances.

Paul could

    rejoice in tribulation

        sing in a prison cell

            help a jailer who had flogged him

                write several great books from prison.

Furthermore, the apostle could stand unafraid while he addressed some of the wise philosophers of ancient Athens. This man had what it takes.

He was confident, but his confidence was in God. He believed he could do anything and accomplish anything that God wanted him to do.

The Source and the Accomplishment

Add it all up. Confidence, excitement, zeal, inner motivation, positive thinking, accomplishment of goals, and any way you add, the total is the same—SUCCESS.

Since Paul had no books about success or motivation to read, where do you suppose he received his ideas? Here's a starter. He received his ideas from the One who knows more about success and accomplishment than any other—God. Paul learned from the Holy Spirit of God who dwelt in his life. When the source of a success-image is right, then the accomplishment is right. Check Philippians 3:12–14 for accomplishment.

Not that I have already obtained it, or have already become perfect, but I press on in order that I may lay hold of that for which I was laid hold of by Christ Jesus. Brethren, I do not regard myself as having laid hold of it yet; but one thing I do, forgetting what lies behind and reaching forward to what lies ahead, I press on toward the goal for the prize of the upward call of God in Christ Jesus.

Not that I have already obtained it— humility. It shows that Paul viewed achievement as an ongoing process.

But one thing I do—goal-setting. He had written it down. He had taken the purposes of his life and narrowed them into one. We can see the big aim of Paul's life, the main drive, the ultimate passion.

Forgetting what lies behind—refusal to dwell on the negatives. If looking back could ever ruin someone, Paul was the one. He had persecuted the church, made havoc of God's work, held the coats of those who had stoned Stephen, and had been a leader in the first-century hatred movement. Sins and sorrows had to be forgotten, or success would have fled.

Reaching forward to what lies ahead—exciting enthusiasm about opportunities just ahead.

I press on—burning desire.

toward the goal—discipline, dedication, a fixed purpose.

for the prize—that winning feeling. Paul believed he couldn't help but be successful if he could continually be the person God wanted him

to be and continually achieve the goals God wanted him to achieve.
of the upward call of God in Christ Jesus—setting of priorities.
And that's what it takes to produce a real success image.

Characteristics of a Biblical Success Image

Christianity has well remembered some of the sterling characteristics of the apostle Paul. His best known qualities have been cited for centuries.

APPRECIATIVE—
"I thank my God in all remembrance of you" (Phil. 1:3).
CONCERNED—
"For I could wish that I myself were accursed,
separated from Christ for the sake of my brethren, my
kinsmen according to the flesh" (Romans 9:3).
CONSIDERATE—
"Therefore, if food causes my brother to stumble, I will never
eat meat again, that I might not cause my brother to stumble"
(I Cor. 8:13).
HUMBLE—
". . . to me, the very least of all the saints" (Eph. 3:8).
SERVANTLIKE—
"Paul, a bondservant of Christ Jesus" (Rom. 1:1).

But little is said about the other characteristics which made the man. Other things to be considered include at least fifteen additional personal strengths.

BOLD—
"We had the boldness in our God to speak to you..."
(I Thess. 2:2).

CONFIDENT—
"I can do all things through Him who strengthens me" (Phil. 4:13).

COURAGEOUS—
"I opposed him (Cephas or Peter) to his face, because he was to be condemned" (Gal. 2:11).

DETERMINED—
When stoned and left for dead, Paul got up and headed for the next town to preach again (Acts 14:19).

EXCITED—
He was persuaded that nothing could ever separate him from the love of God (Rom. 8:3839).

FOLLOWER OF FAITH INSTEAD OF FEELINGS—
In the midst of a 14-day storm at sea, he exclaimed,—"Keep up your courage, men, for I believe God"
(Acts 27:25).

GOAL-SETTER—
After three missionary journeys, Paul still wanted to go to Rome and later to Spain to carry on his work
(Rom. 15:24).

JOYFUL—
When he looked forward to going to Rome, where he knew he might die, Paul said, "That I may come to you in joy by the will of God and find refreshing rest in your company" (Rom. 15:32).

MOTIVATOR OF OTHERS—
To Philemon he wrote, "Having confidence in your obedience I wrote to you" (Philemon 21).

PERSISTENT—
Two years, while a captive of Rome, living in his own house, apparently being guarded all the time, Paul continued "preaching the kingdom of God" (Acts 28:3031).

POSITIVE THINKER—
"If God is for us, who is against us" (Rom. 8:31).

RADIANT—
"I shall remain and continue with you all for your progress and joy in the faith, so that your proud confidence in me may abound in Christ Jesus" (Phil.1:25-26). Twenty-five times in his letters Paul talks of his joy.

SATISFIED WITH POSSESSIONS—
"I have learned to be content in whatever circumstances I am" (Phil.4:11). "I have received everything in full, and have an abundance" (v. 18).

THRILLED—
"I have fought the good fight, I have finished the course, I have kept the faith; in the future there is laid up for me the crown of righteousness" (2 Tim. 4:7,8).

VICTORIOUS—
"The Lord will deliver me from every evil deed, and will bring me safely to His heavenly kingdom" (2 Tim. 4:18).

I know many of those qualities are listed in our modern flurry of success books. And I'm delighted. I just consider it important that we remember these ideas originated with Someone else—Someone who was wonderfully in charge of giving daily direction to an apostle's life 2,000 years ago.

GETTING POSITIVE TOO SOON

There isn't a pessimistic note in the New Testament after the resurrection.
—Andrew Blackwood

Well then, is it the power of positive thinking that is required? . . . While, in general, it is good to be optimistic, that optimism must have some basis in fact to be of any help at all.
—Ray Stedman

Don't draw the wrong conclusion from Paul's life. Someone could surmise, "If I could simply teach myself to master positive thinking, I'll have it made." As if that was all there was to it.

A mountain of material has been written about positive thinking, but legitimate questions still arise. Paul's strength at this point could get most anybody excited, but it also brings out questions. For instance, how does positive thinking relate to negative commands? Is the Bible a positive book or is it negative? Are there problems related to positive thinking? Does it always work? How could Paul always be so positive?

Negatives with a Purpose

God's negatives all have a purpose. Every "thou shalt not" is designed to bless the life. The purpose of all God's negatives is positive!

In order to build a positive person, God must teach us to be realistic. There are not just good things in life—there are bad things as well. So there must not just be "do's," but there must also be "don'ts."

The Chase

When God says, "thou shalt not," He is not saying we may not. Nor is He saying we cannot, but He is simply saying we must not if we want to lead a positive life. The All-Wise God is charting a course.

The disciplined distance runner must memorize well his "thou shalt not's." These, however, are not his main concern. His eye must be on the tape! He wants to be the first to cross the finish line! But he trains and disciplines himself to always be aware of the "thou shalt not's." He must not look at his feet. He must not burn himself out on the first lap. He must not look back every second to see how the other guy is doing! He can best think positively only when the right negatives are an ingrained part of his thinking.

Why are there negatives in the Bible? (1) Because of the reality of sin and the danger of it. (2) To tell the truth in love. (3) To simulate common problems that humanity will face.

A simulation expert sat beside me on a flight high over Chicago. Being totally ignorant of his field, I probed a bit. His firm contracted themselves to high schools or technical schools and taught simulation. Students became excited, grade averages rose, near-dropouts took interest.

"Give me a definition of that word," I suggested, with pencil in hand. "Simulation takes place when a firm builds a model of a complete larger system, and that model imitates every possible wrong turn the mechanism can take."

"My company will discuss with you what you want done, and then we will build an inexpensive model of your expensive machinery. We then build in every possible malfunction area, and finally we teach you how to train your students to use it and learn from it.

When I had asked my questions of the young company president, and we had discussed my work for a while, I had a silent moment to reflect on the truths I had learned that day. God seemed to drive my thoughts on simulation toward the Bible.

The Bible has specific help for every problem area man has.

For the first time I knew why there were so many Bible stories of people with problems. For the first time I could understand God's reasoning in listing the faults of some otherwise great Bible characters. Now I knew why God persisted in "telling it like it is." The Bible has specific help for every problem area man has. Either (1) the problem area is confronted with a direct command or specific principle which applies, or (2) God gives an account of someone who had a similar problem and shares the results.

So today science uses, as one method of teaching, one of the same methods used centuries ago in the writing of God's Word. And, the young simulation expert suggested, it is definitely one of the best teaching methods ever devised.

The Bible: Both Positive and Negative

When Robert Fulton first introduced his new invention, the steamboat, and was ready to take it on its first trip, plenty of critics crowded on the river bank. Fulton proved them wrong. These critics yelled, "It'll never start. It'll never start." After a lot of clanking and groaning, it started moving down the river. The critics were momentarily quiet. Then they rallied and hollered, "It'll never stop. It'll never stop."[1] There's a lesson in all that. If negatives were all God gave us to live by, our thinking would indeed be warped. We would never get anywhere. But there's more. The Bible is both positive and negative. It is the perfectly balanced Book for a perfectly balanced life. Rightly interpreted and rightly applied, the Word of God will produce a perfectly balanced life. For like life is meant to be, the Bible is:

Negative on sin,

Positive on the Savior.

Negative on self-sufficiency,
> *Positive on Christ-sufficiency.*

Negative on human strength,
> *Positive on divine strength.*

Negative on harmful habits,
> *Positive on helpful habits.*

Negative on a sin-filled life,
> *Positive on a Christ-filled life.*

Negative on doubt,
> *Positive on faith.*

Negative on shortsightedness,
> *Positive on vision.*

When Paul got his sin problem settled and his relationship right with God, he became a very positive individual indeed. Relying on the sufficiency of Christ, Paul was loaded with positive affirmations.

"I can do all things through Him who strengthens me" (Phil. 4:13).

"My God shall supply all your needs according to His riches in glory in Christ Jesus" (Phil. 4:19).

"[God] is able to do exceeding abundantly beyond all that we ask or think" (Eph. 3:20).

"And we know that God causes all things to work together for good to those who love God, to those who are called according to His purpose" (Rom. 8:28).

"If God is for us, who is against us?" (Rom. 8:31).

"For I am convinced that neither death, nor life, nor angels, nor principalities, nor things present, not things to come, nor powers, nor height, nor depth, nor any other created thing, shall be able to separate us from the love of God, which is in Christ Jesus our Lord" (Rom. 8:38-39).

The Bible teaches the kind of positive thinking where one so believes in the power of God to accomplish a task, he moves forward in that power and allows God to work through him in the achievement.

The Main Problem in the Positive Thinking Movement

The whole fallacy of the positive thinking movement is not positive thinking. The fallacy is in getting positive too soon. If we do not get our motivation from God, and put our "success" under God, we might be in for trouble. It is not enough to simply start a day saying, "I'm going to be positive." God may choose not to add His blessings to our human methodology when the same human methodology phased Him out of the planning.

Suppose an unsaved person cons himself into thinking positively about his spiritual condition. Suppose he repeats this fifty times a day, "I'm going to think positively about my spiritual condition." Or suppose he frequently says to himself, "Every day in every way I'm getting better and better!" Does this positive thinking change his relationship to God? Is he or she then God's child?

If a carpenter makes a pulpit stand for a church, can it be said that the pulpit is his child? The piece of furniture is his product, not his child. There's a great deal of difference between being one of God's products and one of God's children. As it would be necessary to be born into the family of a carpenter to be the child of a carpenter, so it is necessary to be born into the family of God to be considered God's child and be a recipient of the blessing He has promised to His children. "You must be born again."

Positive thinking, based on truth, carries fantastic blessing. Getting positive too soon, on the other hand, can do irreparable damage.

When Dr. J. Edwin Orr was speaking in a meeting at the University of Chicago, a young lady's question began a dialogue:

"I don't understand this. If a man believes in Communism, he is a

Communist; if he believes in Socialism, he is a Socialist: well, I believe in Christianity—am I not a Christian?"

"Not necessarily so," I replied.

I noticed that she was wearing an engagement ring, so I asked:

"Could I ask you a personal question?"

"Certainly," she replied.

"Do you believe in marriage?"

"Of course I believe in marriage!" she replied. "I'm engaged to be married."

"Can you give me any good reasons for it?"

"Marriage," she said, "gives a woman a home and a family, a career and social prestige."

Facetiously, I asked the young ladies in the company present how many of them believed in marriage, and they all raised their hands—except one determined girl.

"That's very interesting," said I. "You all say that you believe in marriage as an institution or a philosophy. It so happens that I am a chaplain of the United States Air Force. I am recognized by the state government to perform marriages. This young lady says if one believes in Communism, she is a Communist; if one believes in Christianity, she is a Christian. Now you all tell me you believe in marriage: allow me to pronounce you married."

That was greeted with laughing.

"What's wrong with that?" I asked.

"Mr. Orr," protested one girl, patiently. "You know that marriage is not a philosophy; marriage is a personal relationship!"

"Exactly," I returned. "Christianity is not a mere philosophy; to be a Christian is a personal relationship with Jesus Christ, a living Person."

Why Was Paul So Positive?

Paul seemed to never expect defeat. He always anticipated blessing.

His God was a big God! There was no task too big for God to do!

How can any one man be such a positive thinker? Was he just better than most of us at conjuring up good positive thoughts? Or was there a basis for it? What is the difference?

Positive thinking (the right kind) is based on three essentials: (1) establishing the right relationship with Christ; (2) keeping the relationship right; (3) being filled with the power of God.

Is it any wonder Paul was a positive thinker? Is it any wonder he possessed such a strong success-image? Paul could afford to be a positive thinker because he kept his life constantly measured by those three essentials.

12

MUST WE ALL JUST "ACT AS IF?" DOES REALITY MATTER?

> *Knowing what I do about God's power and God's willingness to help, I keep on struggling with myself and trying to work things out in my own way when He could save me all the anxiety and do it better and easier. I believe God is made sad at the sight of so many of us trying to work things out for ourselves. He longs to help us, but we won't let Him; we won't ask Him.*
> —*Peter Marshall*
> *Former Chaplain of U.S. Senate*

In the world of motivational thinking, many ideas have been tried. Some may wonder, "Is it possible to psyche myself up to new levels of achievement" when I'm dragging low? If I "act as if" I can accomplish things that I really need to accomplish, can I work on my mental state and, by using that method, become a better achiever?

The Risk Is High

In swimming, I either can or I can't. A thousand times I may tell myself, "I know I can swim." If I psyche myself, if I act as if I can when I can't, and jump into the deep water anyway, I may drown.

In war, I can rush the enemy who outnumbers me 10 to 1, and all the while be "acting as if" I can defeat them all, but the odds are good that I'll soon be dead.

In sickness, I can psyche myself and act as if I'm okay, and I may get better, but I'm taking a huge risk if I don't treat my symptoms.

The Chase

In breaking a law, whether God's law or man's, I can choose to ignore the reality of it in my life, but much of my joy is lost and I short-circuit many blessings I might have had.

In success and achievement, I can psyche myself into emphasizing how much "I" can accomplish. Yet later, I will realize that my "can-do" attitude will not achieve half of what it could have achieved under God's direction.

It scarcely seems worthwhile to risk your life and your career just because someone said *"acting as if"* would work wonders for you. Maybe they forgot to mention that it only works in some things and then it only works some of the time.

What If I Try It? Try to Psyche Myself Anyway?

You can, but don't!!! There are enough people all around you who have already tried it or seem to be trying it now. Or, you can start with the first three chapters of Genesis and sadly observe Adam and Eve in their attempt to reach their plan of self-sufficiency. Self-sufficiency can, at times, be no more than self-deception. Adam and Eve deceived themselves into thinking their intellectual brain capacities could expand, and they would quickly move into the hall of fame of human greatness. So they *"acted as if"* there should be no permanent rules that would limit them. God had made them free, so they would do what they wanted to do. Result? Adam's own testimony—"I hid myself, I didn't know what else to do about what I had done, so I just went into hiding."[1]

What about you? Maybe you act as if you have more power than you really have. Or you try acting as if you have more knowledge than you have. You could also hear that you ought to ditch your beliefs and moral values and act as if those beliefs and values are just crutches. But the friend who criticized you for having something or Someone to lean on, has probably relied on a house-builder, auto maker, banker, plumber, electrician, auto mechanic, computer expert—all crutches to lean on, if you care to call them by that name. There is great value in leaning on those who have more knowledge in their fields than you do.

Others act as if there is no God, no true Bible, no after-life, no absolute truth, no right or wrong, no standard set of commandments or rules that will fit everyone. (Imagine a parent telling their daughter's date that they believe there are no rules, and there are no standards of right or wrong).

It is interesting that the same people who speak of no absolute truth may expect you to believe that their opinions are absolutely right. Also, where do you get answers about the big questions of life—purpose, grief, sorrow, meaning, morality, love, and destiny?

Remember the same truth stated earlier—In the field of human endeavor, *"acting as if"* only works in some things, and then it may just work part of the time.

Something Better Than Acting

The human body, it has been estimated, may have as many as ten million nerves. Ten million little nerves to get frustrated. Ten million little nerves with frazzled edges looking for a better way than acting. Ten million little nerves stand pleading for an honest way out of frustration, anxiety, and stress.

Dr. Maxwell Maltz, the plastic surgeon/author mentioned in Chapter 3, mentions a startling truth. After years of giving patients new reasons to look in the mirror and like themselves, he found that even after he gives the person a brand new face . . . *"The unhappy, failure-type personality cannot develop a new self-image by pure willpower or by arbitrarily deciding to . . . . You cannot merely imagine a new self-image, unless you feel that it is based upon truth."* [2]

It is imperative we search for a more lasting way than that of faking it till we make it. Our confidence must also come from the inside.

The Chase

Three Basic Laws

Three laws must be understood before we can be assured of success: the law of self-effort, the law of reversed effort, and the law of divine effort.

Law of self-effort—To win a battle, self must be stronger and possess more power than its opponent. If an individual is to be successful as he battles Satan and temptation, then that individual must be stronger than Satan. Otherwise, he cannot hope to win. Satan knows how to defeat everyone who fights with self-effort. He seems to know my every weakness and can, at any moment, hit me at my weakest point. I am simply not always stronger than he is. Analyze the following conversation:

Jesus: "Simon, Satan is after you, really after you."
Simon: "Don't worry about me. I am ready."
Jesus: "If the way you're going to fight him is through self-effort, the big 'I,' then the outcome is already known. You will soon deny Me three times."[3]

Yet self-effort is the way many people fight the battles of life. The longer this self-effort method is used, the more likely the next law will come into play.

Law of reversed effort—If we try too hard not to do something, we will finally do it because we will have impressed it so indelibly upon our minds. Robert Thouless in his book about the psychology of religion discusses this law.

Suppose that you have been told to walk along a plank lying on the floor of the room in which you are at present sitting, without stepping off on

90

either side. You would have very little emotion about the possibility of your failure, and you would accomplish the task quite easily. Now suppose that you have been told that you must walk along something equally rigid and of the same width at a height of several hundreds of feet above the ground. You will almost certainly fall off. What has happened is that your horror of falling off has made the spontaneous autosuggestion of the fall so strong that you have not been able to prevent your mind from realizing it. You will also find, under these conditions, that the harder you try to prevent yourself from falling off, the more certainly you will do so.[4]

James Jauncey adds, "Suppose a young man is troubled with impure thoughts which he finds almost impossible to drive from his mind. The more he struggles, the more involved he becomes. Even prayer does not seem to help. What he is doing is making the problem worse by focusing his mind upon it."[5]

Robert Thouless relates how the plank can be walked.

Your only chance of performing the task successfully is to adopt a method which reduces to a minimum both your fear of the fall and your voluntary effort to keep on the plank; in other words, you must think neither about the height nor about the effort necessary to keep on the plank, but only about getting to the other end.[6]

Law of Divine Effort—God's power is the strongest power that exists, and it is divine power that can meet any need or master any situation. Oswald Chambers, in his excellent book, *My Utmost for His Highest*, must have been thinking about this law.

A river is victoriously persistent; it overcomes all barriers. For a while it goes steadily on its course, then it comes to an obstacle and for a while it is baulked, but it soon makes a pathway round the obstacle. Or a river will drop out of sight for miles, and presently emerge again broader and grander than ever. You can see God using some lives, but into your life an obstacle has come and you do not seem to be of any use. Keep paying attention to the Source, and God will either take you round the obstacle or remove it. The river of the Spirit of God overcomes all obstacles. Never get your eyes on the obstacle or the difficulty. The obstacle is a matter of indifference to the river which will flow steadily through you if you remember to keep right at the Source. Never allow anything to come between yourself and Jesus Christ, no emotion, or experience: nothing must keep you from the one great sovereign Source.[7]

Divine effort, when applied, stops all possibility of failure due to overworked self-effort. Honesty demands that we admit that there are some things we cannot do, some battles we cannot win, some goals we cannot achieve. Many a Christian has made the mistake of attempting to master self-effort and failing to zero in on Divine effort.

The Bible does not just say, "Resist the devil, and he will flee from you," yet that's the way many people quote it. That would simply be self-effort at its futile best. It would be far better to memorize the entire verse: "Submit therefore to God. Resist the devil and he will flee from you."[8]

Submission, turning the problem over to God, enables divine effort to be applied, and Satan knows to flee from that. Satan knows when he has met his match. When he finds a person who turns him over to the Lord, Satan knows he will be defeated.

Anxious that we move ahead to victory, God inspired several of His writers to teach us this same law of divine effort.

Paul: "Put on the full armor of God, that you may be able to stand firm against the schemes of the Devil."[9]

Isaiah: "Though youths grow weary and tired, and vigorous young men stumble badly, yet those who wait for the Lord will gain new strength; they will mount up with wings like eagles, they will run and not get tired, they will walk and not become weary. [10]

John: "Greater is he who is in you than he who is in the world." [11]

Remember—Satan is the prince of this world. Self-effort is not sufficient to fight the biggest battle of all—the battle of life. At best, self-effort will sooner or later fail; at worst, self-effort will become reversed effort. True success is seeking and discovering God's Divine effort and His Divine work in us.

PART FOUR:

Discovering the Secret

13

CHRISTIANITY IS A RELATIONSHIP

When I became a Christian, Jesus Christ came to live in my heart in the person of His Holy Spirit. Real Christianity is really Christ-in-you-ity.
—John Hunter

We are not saved to go to heaven. If so, why didn't we go to heaven right then? Heaven is a by-product. We were saved to tell others and to let Jesus Christ live in us.
—Jimmy Draper

One reason the average person never dreams of relating success and spirituality is that his basic understanding of Christianity is wrong. When he or she defines Christianity correctly, they will come to value their spiritual life more than ever before. You will even see it as the secret to a successful life.

If you were assigned the task of defining Christianity in a sentence or two, how would you go about it?

A pastor friend was in my town, and he shared a concern with me. He said that he had been asked to write a paper on the meaning of Christianity that would receive nationwide distribution.

"Bill, my problem is that I don't know how to begin. I'm to write for the new believer, and the assignment is to say it simply, so a person can understand it regardless of their background."

"Have you considered that Christianity can be defined in one word?" I asked. "One word?" he queried. "What would that be?"

The word I suggested to my friend is *relationship*. Christianity is vastly different from all religious systems. It is set apart as totally unique, for Christianity is a relationship—a relationship between two people.

97

The Chase

One is you, and the other is Jesus Christ.

My friend seemed to become excited. "That's exactly right!" he exclaimed. "Any man can understand that."

Difficulty Explained

Maybe the problem began because we have wanted to define Christianity by what it does or has rather than what it is. Check some of the answers you would possibly obtain if you spot-checked with a man-on-the-street interview.

"Christianity is a set of doctrinal beliefs," the first man might remark. Oh great, that means nobody can understand it unless he has taken a number of Bible courses. No, Christianity has doctrinal beliefs, but Christianity is a relationship.

"Christianity is being good to your neighbor," a second man explains. That's good thinking, but not a good definition for Christianity. Certainly no other teacher ever gave such a high concept of neighborliness as did Jesus. He said, "Thou shalt love thy neighbor as thyself." However, being a good neighbor is a fruit of the Christian life, not the root.

"Christianity is love," the third man comments. "God is love," the Bible says, and that's the understatement of the first century. According to Jesus the two great commandments are about love—love to God, and love to your neighbor. "We love because He (God) first loved us." Love gets right at the heart of Christianity. The Christian does love, but that definition would only serve to confuse people. The ancient Greeks had three words which twenty-first-century man might translate as "love": (1) *eros*—sensual, erotic type of love; (2) *filia*—brotherly love, or the friendship kind; (3) *agape*—the Godlike kind of love. If by definition, Christianity is love, some will never understand because their concept of love is scrambled.

The fourth "man on the street" says Christianity is just another religion. Not so. Christianity is quite different from all other religions.

For the purpose of filling out forms it will no doubt be classified as a religion from now until Jesus comes, but this cannot be how Christianity is defined.

Religion: A group of teachings designed to tell a person how to live, designed by a leader who can furnish no power to enable a follower to live up to the teachings.

Christianity: A relationship to a living Person who has not only provided a group of teachings about how to live, but who indwells His follower so as to provide continual power to live the suggested life.

Christianity is more than a religion. It's a personal relationship!

The Descriptions of Jesus

Calling Christianity a relationship will explain some of the simple statements of Jesus. "Follow Me" (Matt. 16:24) was His way of saying, "Let's start the relationship." Those who receive Him are said to be sons of God (John 1:12). "You must be born again" (John 3:7) also speaks of the initiation of a relationship. Born once, a man is related to his parents in a relationship as close as life itself. Born again, a man is related to Jesus. Born once, man has a nature that soon tends toward sin. Born again, man gains another nature, one that is Godlike. Born once, he is a son of Adam. Born again, he is a son of God. Born once, man is an heir of his earthly parents. Born again, he is an heir of God and a joint-heir with Jesus Christ.

The relationship idea also helps to clarify verses where Jesus uses metaphors, verses such as "I am the bread of life" and "I am the living bread which came down from heaven. And "He who believes in Me, as the Scripture said, from his innermost being shall flow rivers of living water."[1] When the relationship is established and the relationship is

The Chase

right, there will be an automatic source of flowing power coming from within that person's life—His power.

Another of those metaphors—"For whosoever shall do the will of God, the same is my brother, and my sister, and mother"[2] suggests that the one who follows Jesus maintains the closest possible relationship to Him, a relationship as close as that of a mother and child.

> **Christianity is more than a religion.**
> **It's a personal relationship!**

The Necessity of Surrender

Some wonder why intellectual believers (possessing only head belief) are not saved. If there is no heart belief (surrender and personal commitment to Christ as Savior and Lord), there is no relationship. It is possible to have been baptized, confirmed, consecrated, and received into a local church and still have no power for life. Only the one who has repented of sin and been born again by personal faith in Jesus Christ can claim to have a personal relationship with Him.

Even devils in hell have an intellectual religion, the Bible says. And that with the true God! "You believe that God is one. You do well: the demons also believe, and shudder." (James 2:19, NASB). The biting sarcasm of James 2:19 suggests, "You even believe in God [you have head belief]? Congratulations! You have now advanced to the same stage as the devils in hell!"

But I believe in God.
So do the devils in hell.
I even believe God had a son named Jesus.
So do the devils in hell.
But I even believe Jesus died to save sinners.
So do the devils in hell.

But I know Jesus does save sinners.
So do the devils in hell.
I even know I'm a sinner.
So do the devils in hell.

But there is one place the comparison stops! When a person who intellectually believes, takes one step farther and repents and yields his life to Christ, Christ will initiate a personal relationship with that person. The devils come to a screeching halt at that point—they rebel and tremble.

The Power of the Relationship

"I'm in the ditch," the man pleaded. "Help me!"

"Here is a list of seven steps," the Buddhist said kindly. "If you follow these, you will have a good life."

"I can tell you which direction to face if you want to pray while you're in that ditch," the Muslim commented. "If you want out, pray in the right direction."

Several others walked by and offered suggestions, and the man was all ears. He appreciated the advice, but he was powerless to get out.

Until Jesus came by.

"If you want Me to, I will come down to where you are, put My strength into your body, and with My power in you, together we'll come out of that ditch!"

Christianity is a personal relationship between two people in which One person provides the power to meet the other person's needs. Religion cannot provide that power, but Jesus Christ can.

The Promise of a Continued Relationship

Jesus chose some disciples and related Himself personally to each one, and they liked that . . . until the week came for Jesus to die. The disciples came unglued. Sensing they were shaken, Jesus calmed them with the following words, "Let not your heart be troubled."[3] In essence He was saying, "I have been related to you, but it's not all over. I will come again and receive you. And if you're wondering what will happen in the meantime—I've provided for that too. I will not leave you comfortless—I will come to you. How? Let Me tell you about the Holy Spirit" (see John 14:1–3, 16–18).

Through the Holy Spirit, the relationship Jesus had initiated with the disciples would wonderfully continue. They would have with them, wherever they went, the secret to a successful life.

THE HOLY SPIRIT: WHO HE IS AND WHAT HE DOES

You are going to make history with even greater success stories than those written about me.
—Jesus Christ [1]
Two extremes have developed about the Holy Spirit. "If I think of being Spirit-filled," the average believer concludes, "I will either (1) lose all confidence, or (2) be expected to act half-crazy." As long as Satan can keep him thinking that way, he has the man where he wants him—not desiring to be filled with God's fullness and not having God's power for his everyday practical life.
—whc

Time: the last week of the earthly life of Jesus.

Place: Jerusalem

Setting: Jesus, speaking to His disciples, seeks to prepare them for the cross.

Jesus was about to conclude a three-year ministry, the deeds of which would still be shared with thousands of people twenty centuries later, During these three years the crowds had discovered that Jesus was:

Confident

A personality who drew great crowds

A dreamer

A master motivator

An extraordinary goal-achiever

Filled with the power of God

Loaded with love,

103

The Chase

Yet bold and brave.

Jesus' subject matter in this last conversation with His disciples prior to the cross concerns two things: (1) the Holy Spirit, and (2) success.

The success they would achieve would be gigantic. "He who believes in Me, the works that I do shall he do also; and greater works than these shall he do; because I go to the Father" (John 14:12).

The disciples simply sat amazed, wondering how. Jesus continued and explained that The Holy Spirit "abides with you, and will be in you" (v. 17). Jesus was saying, "You will be programmed for success. I have no doubt you will achieve it."

The person and power of the Holy Spirit was programmed to become a part of every born-again believer's life.

The Third Major Invasion

Since the days of creation there have been three distinct major invasions—three unique ways God has shared His power with the human race.

The first invasion—when
God invaded creation to walk
with the Adams and the Enochs.

The second invasion—the
birth of Jesus. God had
invaded history to put His
Son in Jewish clothes.

The third invasion—the indwelling
Holy Spirit. "It is to your advantage that I go away,"
Jesus had related (John 16:7). "But He (the Holy Spirit)
abides with you and shall be in you" (John 14:17).

Paul would later describe Invasion No. 3 as a unique mystery: ". . . the mystery which has been hidden from the past ages and generations, but has now been manifested to His saints, to whom God willed to make known what is the riches of the glory of this mystery among the Gentiles, which is Christ in you, the hope of glory" (Col. 1:26-27).

What a mystery and what a miracle! Born-again believers would have a unique power within—Christ Himself would be dwelling within their lives through the Holy Spirit.

Who Is the Holy Spirit?

He is the key to the relationship.
No key was needed while Jesus was alive. They could see Christ with them, feel His power around them, be assured when He spoke to them, answer questions for them, and lift burdens from them. But if He was not around?

Then they would need Him around. "It is to your advantage that I go away," Jesus said. The purpose of His leaving was so that He, through the Holy Spirit, could be around all the time—with each separate one, in every city, to provide the exact power needed in each situation. When He would be working in many different locations all at once, they would do greater works, reach more people, and achieve more accomplishments in His name than Jesus had done during the short years of His ministry.

He is the source of real power.
The Old Testament prophet had revealed remarkable truth—"Not by might, nor by [human] power, but by My spirit, says the Lord" (Zech. 4:6). Jesus had reemphasized it to the disciples. "But you shall receive power when the Holy Spirit has come upon you" (Acts 1:8). The book of Acts explodes with the punch of power. The disciples denied it was their power (3:12), but they insisted it was the power of the Holy Spirit producing the miracles (4:7-8). Check the source of Stephen's power (6:3, 8). Or hear Peter's explanation of why Jesus had power— "You know of Jesus of Nazareth, how God anointed Him with the Holy Spirit

and with power" (10:38).

The Holy Spirit is also Christ in you!

Jesus spoke of the Holy Spirit saying, "He abides with you, and will be in you" and following that statement He immediately said, "I will come to you" (John 14:17-18). The coming One was Jesus, but now Jesus was coming through the Holy Spirit rather than in physical form. He would be another Helper (John 14:16). In the Greek language "helper" means another of exactly the same kind.

Other Bible descriptions of the Divine Motivation Expert are:

"If Christ is in you" (Col. 1:27).

"If Christ be in you." (Rom. 8:10)

"His Spirit who indwells you" (Rom. 8:11)

"If anyone does not have the Spirit of Christ" (Rom. 8:9).

". . . the Spirit of Him who raised Jesus from the dead
    dwells in you" (Rom. 8:11)

"Christ lives in me" (Gal. 2:20).

"For to me, to live is Christ" (Phil. 1:21).

"Christ, who is our life" (Col. 3:4).

Harold Wildish asks, "Did you hear of the three men who claimed ownership of the same house?"

"I bet they had a fuss over that."

"No, not at all. The first man was the builder of the house. He planned the whole thing and put it up for sale. The second man was the buyer who now is the owner. He has rented it to the tenant who now resides there."

"God the Father made it. God the Son with His precious blood redeemed it, bought it at Calvary; God the Holy Spirit has come to reside within." Then Wildish comments, "Surely the God who made, redeemed, and possessed man would be sufficient to make him the victorious Christian he longed to be."[2]

Every believer has the Holy Spirit but comparatively few have found the secret of His unusual power for daily living.

The Work of the Holy Spirit

The Holy Spirit (1) establishes the relationship; (2) enforces the rules; (3) enriches the life; (4) empowers for service. At the time of salvation the personal relationship is established. The Holy Spirit enters, and He is "with you" and "in you" (John 14:17). In fact, "if anyone does not have the Spirit of Christ, he does not belong to Him" (Rom. 8:9).

Enforcing the rules (teaching) is another vital part of the work of the Holy Spirit within. Jesus said, "He [the Holy Spirit] will teach you [the believer] all things" (John 14:26). Many methods of teaching are used, but one of the more noticeable methods is "disciplining" (see Heb. 12:6–7). God disciplines when necessary, but only to teach the believer to be a better child next time. When the teaching is over and the sin has been confessed, the believer is free to move on to better things.

Enriching the life is no less important in the Holy Spirit's work. Even as Jesus spoke to the disciples of the Holy Spirit, He promised fantastic peace. There would be no need for them to be troubled or afraid (John 14:27). Furthermore, the life would be fruitful. Dawson Trotman suggested the Christian is "born to reproduce." Jesus said, "I chose you, and appointed you, that you should go and bear fruit" (John 15:16). But that's not all! After speaking to them about the Holy Spirit, He told them why—"These things I have spoken to you, that . . . your joy may be made full" (John 15:11).

Empowering the believer is perhaps the greatest work of all. Every believer has the Holy Spirit (Rom. 8:9) but comparatively few have found the secret of His unusual power for daily living.

But the subject of the Holy Spirit's role in providing power demands a chapter by itself.

FILLED WITH GOD'S FULLNESS

The road to success is always under construction.
—whc

Being filled with the Spirit is an inside job. If you insist on
an outer experience, then you make emotions the king.
—Jack R. Taylor

Years ago someone stated, "I used to think a few men had a monopoly on the power of the Holy Spirit. I have since learned the Holy Spirit has a monopoly on a few men."

The believer cannot be as successful as God intends, cannot have the peace, joy and abundant life God desires for him, unless he comes to understand what it is to "be filled with the Spirit." The purpose of this chapter is to lead the believer to enjoy the Spirit-filled or Christ-controlled life.

But first let's analyze three little verbs. Analysis of negative reactions will hopefully lead toward application of a positive command, the end result being the achievement of power within.

Negative Reactions Toward the Holy Spirit

"You are always resisting the Holy Spirit" (Acts 7:51).
"Do not quench the Spirit" (1 Thess. 5:19).
"And do not grieve the Holy Spirit" (Eph. 4:30).
Many never discover the joy God desires for them to possess. Why? Some resist God's Spirit, others quench God's Spirit, and still others grieve Him. What's the difference?
Resisting the Holy Spirit is an act performed by an unsaved person.

When this verb is used, Stephen is speaking to unsaved people who were resisting (or fighting off) the Spirit of God as He was convicting their hearts of sin. Even as Stephen shared, they resisted.

The unsaved person has many ways he can resist the Holy Spirit because there are many ways God calls him. Sometimes God speaks through his goodness (Rom. 2:4); sometimes through a concerned relative or friend (John 1:40–41); sometimes through trouble (Acts 16:25–34); sometimes through a sermon (1 Cor. 1:21); sometimes through a Bible verse (2 Tim. 3:15); and sometimes through a still small voice (1 Kings 19:9–12). And sometimes God uses all of these ways to get our attention! When God speaks, regardless of the method He chooses, the unsaved person either receives or resists. If he resists, he never receives the joy God has for him.

Do not quench the Spirit is Paul's statement to the Thessalonians in a letter written shortly after he left the city in A.D. 54. Undoubtedly he was writing to many new Christians. God impelled him to remind them "do not quench the Spirit." Quench means to "extinguish or cool suddenly." Every new believer faces this danger in the first few months of being a Christian. While the conversion experience is still fresh, Satan whispers, "You didn't mean that. That was a moment of emotion. Don't do anything else about it." To fail to obey God's direct commands and to follow God's leadership is to "quench the Spirit." Again, joy flees.

Do not grieve the Holy Spirit was the negative used in Ephesians. David Smith, in *Life and Letters of St. Paul,* suggests that the three years Paul spent in Ephesus were from A.D. 53–56. But it was A.D. 62, six years later, when Paul wrote back for the first time. Paul's converts had been saved at least six years!

Grieving speaks of a heretofore close relationship, established over a period of time. We grieve only those we know intimately. We grieve the Holy Spirit because we have walked closely with Him in days gone by. Sin grieves the One who cares the most about us.

"Grieving" occurs when we (1) revert from a Christ-controlled life to a self-controlled life, (2) seem content with second best in our choices, and (3) expect God to do little or nothing through us (and we give Him just that much opportunity!). It is sad indeed when a believer spurns God's love and grieves the Holy Spirit.

The Positive Command for the Believer

"Resist not," "quench not," and "grieve not" share only the negative side. On the positive side, the command is "be filled with the Spirit." "Grieve not the Holy Spirit," Paul commands, and then he quickly adds: "Be filled with the Spirit" (Eph. 4:30; 5:18).

The sidetracks which divert our attention from "being filled" are astonishing. Some people would mistakenly have us searching for "the gift of the Holy Spirit." However, the gift of the Spirit is received at the moment of salvation (Acts 2:38). In fact, "If anyone does not have the Spirit of Christ, he does not belong to Him" (Rom. 8:9). It is in the conversion experience, through the act of faith, that we receive the gift of the Holy Spirit (Gal. 3:13–14). Simply put, we receive the wonderful gift of having Him live in our lives to give help, direction, and power.

Others suggest a "Holy Spirit baptism" is needed. True, Jesus had suggested to His disciples they would be "baptized with the Holy Spirit, but He added, "not many days from now" (Acts 1:5). On the day of Pentecost His prophecy was fulfilled. They were baptized (immersed or covered with) the power of God's Holy Spirit (Acts 2). After Acts 2, the Bible takes a new turn—a dramatic switch in terminology. And there is a reason—Pentecost, as a day or as a happening, did not need to be repeated. God had immersed His young church with power. God had done exactly what He had wanted and promised to do on that day.

For those who live on this side of Pentecost, there is a new emphasis.

Acts 4:8   "Then Peter, filled with the Holy Spirit . . ."
Acts 4:31   "And they were all filled with the Holy Spirit."

The Chase

Acts 6:3   "Seven men . . ., full of the Holy Spirit and wisdom . . ."

Acts 6:5   "Stephen, a man full of faith and the Holy Spirit . . ."

Acts 7:55 "But being full of the Holy Spirit, he [Stephen] gazed intently into heaven . . ."

Acts 11:24 "He was a good man, and full of the Holy Spirit and of faith."

Acts 13:9 "Paul, filled with the Holy Spirit . . ."

The divine imperative is for us to be filled with the Spirit.

Wonderfully Practical

When the Bible commands us to be filled with the Spirit (Eph. 5:18), and when it suggests we be filled with all the fullness of God (Eph. 3:19), the result is the same. We are simply to be so related to the One within that He is captain and Lord of our life.

He wants not just to be resident, but also President.

He wants not just to be living within, but to be Lord within.

He desires not just to be Messiah, but to be Master.

God is suggesting He knows more about how to run a life than any one of us. He longs that we be filled with His fullness.[1]

How To Be Filled Each Day

The real issue is, "Can God be trusted?" If He can, we should stake our whole lives on Him.

When a life is self-controlled, it possesses only the power that can be generated by self. When a life is Christ-controlled, the unlimited power supply of God is always available.

For Christ to control the life, the believer must daily crown Jesus

Lord of his or her life. The process could be remembered by the three C's.

(1) **Confess** every known sin and ask His forgiveness, claiming His promise of cleansing in 1 John 1:9.

(2) **Crown** Jesus Lord of your life each day, by an act of volition and by telling Him so. Ask Him to show you those places in your life which you have heretofore petitioned off (acting as if you knew more about life than He did).

(3) **Claim** His fullness according to His promise in 1 John 5:14–15.

It is very important that the three C's become a daily practice. The calm quiet of the prayer closet each morning can lead the believer to experience the abundant joy of the Spirit-filled life. With Jesus crowned Lord of life, the believer moves to face the day with excitement. Not self, but Jesus Christ is now in charge.

Someone could ask, "Does the concept of the Spirit-filled life teach a doctrine of perfection? Not at all. In fact, it teaches exactly the opposite. It teaches the Bible doctrine of imperfection by showing the need to crown Jesus Lord of our lives every day anew.

Reason dictates that a life with Christ in charge (a life filled with the Holy Spirit) could produce a dramatic change in the power to achieve.

Suppose Christ was in charge of your life today and you were confident of that one fact. Results?

(1) You could now enjoy living with yourself. And this time you can forego the ego-bit. Christ would be the power behind the life, not you.

(2) You could rejoice more, trusting problems to Him. After all, now your problems belong to the One in charge.

(3) You could expect the power of God as you daily confront tough situations.

(4) You could thrill to bigger goals, knowing He is able to do

exceeding abundantly above all that we ask or think (Eph. 3:20).

(5) You could meet each temptation with prayer, thanking Him that "greater is He who is in you [Jesus Christ] than he who is in the world [Satan]"(1 John 4:4). This would be the same as saying, "Lord, I cannot win this fight, but You can. I am not greater than Satan, but You are. I am trusting You to be my victory."

SELF-IMAGE; CHRIST-IMAGE

Success is expected in God's children (Josh. 1:8), but nowhere does the Bible even hint that self-power is the power that brings it to pass.
—whc

Christianity is a science, a deep science, which tries to do away with the evil or the fall into selfishness by substituting for self the Son of God, which is Christ.
—F. B. Meyer

A college boy texted home saying,
"Mom, have failed everything, Prepare Pop."
The boy received this reply the next day:
"Pop prepared. Prepare yourself."

There's the toughest battle of all. Most of us have our biggest problem in getting self-prepared. By the way, how do you go about that?

Two Natures

A counselor may suggest, "Get a good appreciation for the kind of person you are—the kind of person God made you."

Analyze that suggestion. Is it possible? If you get such appreciation of yourself, can you maintain it?

(1) You desperately want to appreciate yourself.
(2) You sometimes thoroughly appreciate what you see.
(3) Other times you know you are not what God made you to be—hence you cannot appreciate yourself.

The Chase

It is important to understand that the believer has two natures. One nature is displeasing to the Lord. The other nature is made in His likeness. The first is the self-nature, or fleshly nature. The second is the new nature, the Christ-like nature.

When I have unconfessed sins in my life, and have made no attempt to confess them to Christ, I am allowing the carnal, fleshly nature to rule. When the old nature is ruling in my life, I just simply cannot be satisfied with myself, try as I may. Nor should I be. I have enough inner sensitivity to tell me that however God made me, that's not the way He did it. I've been interfered with!

Rather than admit there's a self I can't stand, I go into the business of excusing myself—as if God didn't know me better than that. A Tulsa newspaper carried a classic example:

Judge Gets Verdict by Mail

WICHITA, KAN. (AP)—The blizzard this week forced everyone to cope with unusual circumstances.

One Wichita man was scheduled to appear in Municipal Court Tuesday with a speeding charge. The court was closed because of the heavy snow, and the following letter arrived in the court clerk's office Friday:

"I was scheduled to be in court February 23, at 12:15 P.M. concerning a traffic ticket. Well, I was there as scheduled. And to my surprise I was the only one there. No one called and told me that court would be closed.

"After going through the snow to be there on time, I decided to go ahead with the hearing as scheduled, which meant that I had to be the accuser (the patrolman who gave me the citation), and I had to be the accused and also the judge.

"The citation was for going 46 miles per hour in a 35 mile per hour zone. I had the speed alert on my car set on 44 miles per hour. As the accuser I felt that I was going over 35 miles per hour, but as the accused I knew that I was not going 46 miles per hour and as the judge, and being the understanding man that I am, I decided to throw it out of court this time, but it had better not happen again."

In confession of sin, two extremes are possible. Guard against these:

1. Act as if there is little or nothing to confess. Unconfessed sin leads to a guilt complex.

2. Morbid introspection. This person sees more than God sees.

The psalmist had a simple but excellent plan. On his knees in prayer, he asked God to reveal things to him—"Search me, O God, and know my heart: try me, and know my thoughts: and see if there be any wicked way in me" (Ps. 139:23). If you ask God to reveal things in you that are displeasing to Him, you can bet He will!

Fallacy of the Self-Controlled Man

Sit down and brace yourself. You may need to think on this one a while. But if the Bible is true, then there is no such thing as a totally self-controlled man.

Not that man doesn't want to be, try to be, and hope to be, but as it works out—he doesn't get to be. There's someone out to make certain man doesn't control himself.

1. Satan is out to ruin our lives by usurping control (1 Pet. 5:8).
2. Satan does not expect to fail. He has never failed completely except with one person—Jesus Christ (Heb. 4:15).

3. Every other person who has ever lived has done Satan's bidding (sin) at some time or another (Rom. 3:10, 23).
4. Since Satan has proved himself stronger than all of us, we can correctly assume he is stronger than self.
5. Therefore no one is completely self-controlled, for at times Satan is in control, persuading us to disobey God.

That trickster! Before a person sins, he is heard to say—"I can do whatever I want to do!" Afterward comes the remorseful—"I don't know why I did that—that wasn't what I wanted!" Instead of self-control, that's Satan-control! The one who starts out as a "I want to run my own life" person invariably winds up as a "Something is ruining my life" person. That's how powerful Satan is.

Sin is not s-i-n. It is s-I-n. Sin is the big "I"—the big drive of self to control the life. The big "I" sees to it there's not much time for God.

Inferiority Complex?

"But I don't like all this new talk I am hearing about 'self.' There's nothing wrong with self, is there? If I can't have a good self-image, won't I have a terrible inferiority complex?"

Two areas are of immediate concern: (1) Does man have trouble with himself? (2) Will a Christ-controlled life rather than a self-controlled life lead to an inferiority complex?

Does Man Have Trouble with Himself?

Dwight L. Moody, the famed evangelist, admitted, "I have more trouble with myself than any other man I've ever met."

Bible characters seem to honestly admit they had trouble with themselves. And they were great men!

Job	"Then Job answered the Lord and said, "Behold I am insignificant" (Job 40:4).
David	"For I know my transgressions, and my sin is ever before me" (Ps. 51:3).
Ezra	"I am ashamed and embarrassed to lift up my face to Thee, my God; for our iniquities have risen above our heads" (Ezra 9:6).
Isaiah	"Woe is me, for I am ruined! Because I am a man of unclean lips" (Isa. 6:5).
Paul	"Christ Jesus came into the world to save sinners, among whom I am foremost of all." (1 Tim. 1:15).

If I have trouble with self, and self sits in the control tower, then I have trouble in the control room!

Jesus startled the first-century world by telling men to deny themselves. "If anyone wishes to come after Me, let him deny himself, and take up his cross, and follow Me" (Matt. 16:24).

Paul recognized that when self was in charge there would be some wrong affections and lusts. He suggested we crucify the flesh. "They that are Christ's have crucified the flesh with the affections and lusts" (Gal. 5:24). Crucifixion is also his descriptive term in Galatians 2:20; 6:14; and Romans 6:6, 11.

When Paul mentioned being "crucified with Christ," he may have been giving you a glance into his prayer life. Paul has been open and honest in Romans 7 when he admitted he still had some big battles with his old nature. Now, in prayer, he may have prayed something like this. "Lord, I'm having a wrestling match with my old nature again. But I have no interest in being just a self-controlled man. I want to be Christ-controlled today and every day. Lord, You be in charge."

Okay, a skeptical Christian asks, "Just suppose I did ask Jesus, every day, to be the Lord of my life and the Lord of my day. Wouldn't that make me feel inferior, give me an inferiority complex?"

The Chase

Will Christ-Control Lead to an Inferiority Complex?

Two things desperately need to be said at this point. If the first idea startles, the second will soothe. If the first troubles, hopefully the second will thrill.

1. The believer is inferior in some areas. He knows he is inferior to the Lord. This is derived from simple honesty. Does it bother him—no! He is thrilled to know there is Someone who has strength he doesn't. He knows he is inferior to the devil. His logic convinced him of this. Having yielded to wrong thoughts or attitudes before, he knows it could happen again. He knows he is inferior at living the Christian life. Since only One has ever lived the Christian life like it should be lived—Jesus Christ—the believer realizes his lack of ability in this area.

2. When Christ is crowned Lord of the life, the believer is not inferior. Nor should he feel inferior. He can refuse to feel defeated, and he has a strong Bible statement to back it up. When Christ is on the throne of his life, he can expect to have fresh power. He can ask himself, "Who is greater?" And the answer comes back—"Greater is He who is in you, than he who is in the world." (I John 4:4). No doubt this includes the prince (KJV) or ruler (NASB) of this world. (see John 12:31, 14:30, 16:11).

Believers should refuse to feel inferior to problems if they are rightly related to Christ. Christ, who is in control now, is greater than those problems. The believer should refuse to feel inferior to anxieties if he is rightly related to Christ. The Christ who lives within is greater than those anxieties, or the thing that brought on the anxieties.

Approach the matter from another direction. The believer is a son of God, a child of the King. Should a child of the King feel inferior? Yes, he should feel inferior to the King. Also, he may rightly feel inferior if he is separated from the power of the King and meets a power stronger than he is.

But those are the only times a child of the King should feel inferior. For any time the power of the King is with him, it would be foolish to have an inferiority complex.

A right relationship each day is vital, since Christ is the power line who supplies the confidence needed for everyday achievement.

Success-Image, Yes; Self-Image, No

So now we come to some important terminology. Should the believer have a success-image? The answer is yes. Remember Paul's built-in success image (Ch. 10)?

However, to say that Paul possessed a great self-image would be misleading. Success-image, yes; but self-image, no.

In chapter 7, success was defined. Success is the continuing achievement of being the person GOD wants you to be and the continuing achievement of established goals God helps you set.

Self-image could be construed to imply that the secret to success is based on self—self's ability to be, and self's ability to do. The Bible would nix that.

Success-image relates to excitement within: (1) Determination that in His power you can be the person God wants you to be; (2) belief that in His power you can achieve the goals He helps you set.

> *A success-image is simply a by-product of getting right and staying right with God.*

The Chase

Toward a Success-Image

Those who desire to move toward a success-image should remember that Paul got his success-image only because he sought a Christ-image.

Seeking to please Christ brought all the wheels of Paul's life into alignment. When his definition was aligned with that of the Lord, and his life was aligned with the wishes of the Lord, and his goals were aligned with those of the Lord, then his success would certainly please the Lord!

Is it any wonder why God chose to bless Paul's life with His power? To possess a failure-image when all of his life's goals were brought into alignment would have been an insult to God.

Now it can be said—a success-image is simply a by-product of getting right and staying right with God!

To be a success, it is imperative to seek—

- ➤ Not more self-control, but more Christ-control.
- ➤ Not more self-centeredness, but more Christ-centeredness.
- ➤ Not more self-esteem, but more Christ-esteem.
- ➤ Not more self-confidence, but more Christ-confidence.
- ➤ Not more self-power, but more Christ-power.
- ➤ Not more self-reliance, but more Christ-reliance

PART FIVE:

Motivated for Action

17

"IF"—THE BIG HINDRANCE TO MOTIVATION

A man is going nowhere as long as he lives in the realm of the conditional. His vocabulary will be full of words like "if," "provided," "in case," "if so," "unless," and "in the event of." Hearing all of these conditional phrases in a person's conversation may well cause you to want to stop and ask, "Sir, is God dead?"
—whc

Why do you say, "If God can use me?" Didn't God use a rod, a jaw-bone, five small stones, a handful of oil and a little meal, five barley loaves and two small fishes?
—whc

A young preacher, preaching at a conference for pastors, shared a tough experience he had faced a few years earlier in his ministry. I had not known him, but from the introduction he received, it became apparent to me God was now using him and blessing his ministry. He said that a few years before, he had been pastoring a small church, nothing exciting was happening, and the thought struck, "If I could just change churches!" In his mind he developed a plan designed to get himself recommended to some other church. He planned how he would do it, which pastor he would approach at their next convention. He also created the answer he would give if that prominent pastor would ask, "How are you doing?"

Scroll forward to that planned hallway meeting. It happened.

"How are you doing?" that pastor asked. "Dr. _____, my church is not going so well, and I don't think I'll ever be able to get those people excited. If you happen to hear of some church in another state which needs a pastor, you might keep me in mind."

Waiting anxiously to hear, "Sure I will. I'll give you a great recommendation," he received the surprise of his life. The highly successful pastor pushed a long finger right toward his face and said, "Let me tell you something, young preacher, and don't you ever forget it. You'll never be happy anywhere until you get happy where you are!"

The young preacher went back to his small, struggling church field, spent a night in prayer on his knees, and dedicated himself to reach the unsaved of that town. And from that moment on, God mightily blessed his ministry.

> *Caution—if anything can keep you from achieving the goals God has for you, it is one word—IF.*

The believer must not allow anything to keep him from God's intended plan of success. He must at all costs be the person God wants him to be, and achieve the goals God wants him to achieve. God's plan for your life must not be sidestepped, for God's plan alone will bring you maximum happiness. No new geographical location will bring it to pass.

Caution—if anything can keep you from achieving the goals God has for you, it is one word—IF.

Twenty-First Century Success Stoppers

The most prevalent word to prevent us from thinking positively— the most prevalent word to damage our effectiveness in being what God wants us to be and achieving what God wants us to achieve is the word IF.

For a person to claim to be rightly related to the Lord and not allow

God to achieve through him is tragic indeed. Yet most of us can readily locate ourselves in the following list:

If only I had time to read my Bible . . .

If I had more power . . .

If I was healthy like he is . . .

If there was something they would ask me to do . . .

If my work didn't make me so tired . . .

If only I had the energy those young people have . . .

If our church wasn't like it is . . .

If I were talented . . .

If those other Christians I know would get on the ball . . .

If my job wasn't so demanding . . .

If my kids would read the Bible and practice it . . .

If I made the money he does . . .

If I could memorize those promises . . .

If I had a better pastor . . .

If God did it like that in our day . . .

If my church had the prospects that the other church has . . .

If I didn't live next door to them . . .

If my husband (wife) loved God more . . .

If I could forgive myself . . .

If I didn't have to go to work so early . . .

If they bragged on me like they brag on him . . .

If only I could have lived when Jesus did . . .

If God didn't have it in for me . . .

If I didn't have to live with my past . . .

If my parents could just understand me . . .

If they ever elect me as a deacon . . .

If my boss didn't have it in for Christians . . .

If I had the training and education he had . . .

If I could speak like the preacher speaks . . .

The Chase

If I had not made that wrong move . . .
If I could have had an easier time growing up . . .
If we ever get to move to a better house . . .
If I had faith like that . . .
If I just knew what to say . . .
If someone would have taught me how to witness when I was
      young . . .

One common bond unites all those excuses. The blame for non-action is elsewhere—never where it belongs.

How many of the twenty-first century success-stopper statements have you used?

The Most Destructive Word

"If" is the word of delay. No inner voice need be totally negative. No one needs to tell us we "cannot" do a task. Enough delay will come through slight implication. "Fine, if you can do it," a voice seems to say. Hearing that thought, we don't even make an attempt.

We are somewhat like the dentist who was bent over working on his patient. The patient in the chair cried, "Here, Doc, you haven't pulled the right tooth!" The dentist replied calmly, "I know it, my good man, but I'm coming to it."

"If" is the word of despair. Delay an action once, and the chances of getting it done diminish. Delay it several times and we may never do it. When God impresses a task upon the mind, and we surrender to some "if," we will be frustrated and in despair.

"If" destroys incentive, wrecks confidence, assassinates character, robs us of God-given dreams, and ruins our adventuresome spirit. Years ago I heard a speaker say...

On the plains of hesitation,
Lie the bleached bones of thousands,

Who, on the very threshold of victory,
Sat down to rest,
And while resting, died.

Great Men Are Not Exempt

One might suspect that great men would be exempt from *if* trouble. Not so. The great servants of God, though plagued with the same problem, move beyond it by trusting the Lord's power to be bigger than the problem (see Eph. 3:20).

If I were Satan, this is the one word I would seek to lodge in the minds of people more than any other, and my major emphasis would be to place it in the minds of God's sharpest servants. The ones most plagued with *if* questions would be the ones God would otherwise most likely use to achieve.

Think how that one word—*if*—must have plagued the prophets. They lived in ancient days, but Satan was alive and well (no, alive and sick) on planet Earth then as now. Imagine with me how the "if" word could have tormented the Old Testament prophets.

Elijah—Shortly after his greatest victory Elijah leaves Mt. Carmel, where the men of Baal have been defeated. He heads for Southern Judah and arrives there extremely tired. After running a good part of the way, Elijah says to himself, "I can win any battle except the battle over Jezebel. *If* only Queen Jezebel had never been born! God, I'm scared. She has her soldiers out to kill me. God, let me die."

Elisha—The same man who has prayed for a double portion of the spirit of Elijah has received it, but he is skeptical as God's power in his life is yet untested. Scared to death, just as he was about to perform his first miracle, he no doubt thought, "*If* only Elijah were alive."

Hosea—God had just shared a tough assignment. "Lord," he must have prayed, "Let me off the hook this time. You know the situation I have at home. I just can't do anything for You. I could and I would be the

129

man You want me to be, *if* only I had a wife who was faithful to me."

Amos—Called to be a prophet while serving in his vocation of gathering sycamore fruit, he pleads with God, "I would be glad to be Your prophet *if* only I had a better education."

Isaiah—God asks, "Whom shall I send, and who will go for us?" The mind of Isaiah receives the temptation to reply, "You know You can always count on me, God. But the other day King Uzziah died. Now the whole nation may fall apart. We're all running a bit scared. *If* only our national affairs were in better shape.

Ezekiel—The brilliant young Jew, captured in Israel and held captive in Babylon, has just been commanded by God to write a book. "I would not mind writing for You, Lord, *if* only I was back in Jerusalem. Talk to me seventy years from now, and *if* we get out of this place, and I'm back home . . ."

Jeremiah—He is being told by God he must preach the truth, even though the people will not appreciate the news of their coming judgment and captivity. For hours Jeremiah wrestles with these thoughts. "I know what I better do. I'll strike a deal with God. I'll tell Him that I'll do it *if* He keeps me out of prison. But *if* I get into trouble and wind up in prison, I'm through listening to God."

Of course the prophets had thoughts like that! They were human, weren't they? Maybe they didn't think those exact thoughts, but in whatever direction they turned they faced the *"if"* scenarios. They became God's giants by refusing to believe those negative thoughts. When God speaks, calls, and assigns, a negative thought must not be tolerated.

Adoniram Judson, an early missionary to Burma, faced seven unbelievably tough years, and in those years can you guess the number of converts he had? None. With a touch of sarcasm a "friend" asked, "What do you think the future holds for your work in Burma?" Judson replied, "The future is as bright as the promises of God!"

"If's" of an Apostle

Since Paul was possibly the greatest Christian since the time of Jesus, one might assume he had no "*ifs*" to overcome. Who said?

The *agnostic* "*if*" was probably Satan's first game with Paul. Atheism doubts with authority but agnosticism doubts by always coming up with more questions. Before the Damascus Road experience, the question marks of agnosticism kept his brain working overtime. "Relax, Paul, you've got a religion. You're a Hebrew of the Hebrews. If Jesus was for real, what could He do for someone with as much religion as you have?"

The *comparison* "*if*" may have been the second thought to get him. "I could never be like Stephen—he was something else. Why, he must have been the greatest Christian there ever was!"

God had no desire for Paul to be like Stephen, or Stephen like Paul! God wanted Paul to be Paul, but a totally yielded Paul.

The *appearance* "*if*" was no doubt his biggest hang-up. There was nothing suave about Paul. His face may have been so common he could not stand himself. Second Corinthians 10:10 (Goodspeed Translation) has Paul quoting back to the Corinthian people the exact crude words they had been saying about him. They had said, "His personal appearance is insignificant and as a speaker he amounts to nothing." The Amplified Translation has the Corinthians' comment, "His personality and bodily presence are weak, and his speech and delivery are utterly contemptible—of no account!" The NASB says his presence is "unimpressive."

Paul could not fake it. Night and day he was tempted to be nervous about his weaknesses. But he believed God could use even the uncommonly common face. It was a case of, "Here I am, God. If You can use me, great. It's up to You. I'm not much. In fact, I'm not anything, but maybe that way You will get all the credit for what's done through my life. Have a go at it, God!"

The *ability* "*if*" was the other half of the Corinthian slur. "As a speaker he amounts to nothing!" The sequence of events may have been—(1) the first night he heard their remark, he wept; (2) the thought came that God could not use him because of his lack of ability; (3) he remembered that God had all power; (4) he realized it was not Paul but "Christ in Paul" which the world desperately needed to see; (5) he determined anew to let Christ use him in whatever way He could; and (6) what God thought about him was the important thing, not what somebody said.

It was A.D. 58 when Paul wrote 2 Corinthians and only two years later (A.D. 60), he was writing to the Colossians saying, "Christ worketh in me mightily" (Col. 1:29). Corinth's comments didn't stop Paul!

Thinking Straight

If . . . if . . . if—ad infinitum. Satan has one "*if*" to cause us to doubt God, another to cause us to doubt God's ability, another to destroy any thought that God could use weak vessels, and on and on it goes.

When a believer is Spirit-filled, however, new thoughts should engulf his brain:

(1) Jesus Christ lives in me.

(2) Jesus, with all the talent and ability He has—lives in me.

(3) Jesus, alive with power, indwells my life through the Holy Spirit.

(4) Jesus has always chosen to do great accomplishments through human vessels, provided they are fit for the Master's use—(2 Tim. 2:15–23).

(5) Jesus can accomplish anything through me—provided I will be clean, forgiven, usable and filled with His fullness. I will choose to ask Him, allow Him, and expect Him to work through me.

One sentence turned Dwight L. Moody on. A speaker said, "The world has yet to see what God can do with one life totally yielded to Jesus Christ." Terrible in speech, poor in grammar, but with a heart hungry to be used, Moody said to himself, "By the grace of God I'll be that man."

> **"The future is as bright as the promises of God!"**

Summary Thoughts

Why wait until all "*ifs*" are removed? At least one "*if*" plagues every person. The greatest Christian you know—or the most handsome—or the most talented—or the greatest achiever—has some feature about himself he would love to see changed. But he relies on God's overcoming grace.

Why should the achiever always be someone else? God has a wonderful plan for your life.

Why should the one little word "*if*" be allowed to destroy the motivation the Holy Spirit has implanted within your life?

18

HOW TO GET MOTIVATED

Real motivation comes from a man knowing where he's going and how he's going to get there. You can see it in a man's eyes when he knows where he's going.
—*W. O. "Bill" Menefee*
Home Care International

For as he thinks within himself, so is he.
Proverbs 23:7

mo'ti-vate (mō'tivāt), v.t. To provide with a motive; to impel; incite. mo'tive (mō'tiv), n. [OF. motif, fr. ML. motivus moving, fr. L. movere, motum, to move] 1. That within the individual, rather than without, which incites him to motion; any idea, need, emotion, or organic state that prompts to an action.

Webster is sharing several basic truths:

(1) Man frequently needs an outside force to move him (implied).
(2) The force which acts from without is not real motivation. It will last for a while but something else must take over.
(3) Real motivation needs to come from within.
(4) Action is the end result of motivation, the goal sought for.

Necessity for the Right Kind of Motivation

Spencer Goodreds tells of an old gentleman riding on the ocean liner. When a storm blew up at sea a young woman, leaning against

135

the ship's rail, lost her balance and was thrown overboard. Immediately another figure plunged into the waves beside her and held her up until a life-boat rescued them. To everyone's astonishment the hero was the oldest man on the voyage—an octogenarian. That evening he was given a party in honor of his bravery. "Speech! Speech!" the other passengers cried.

The old gentleman rose slowly and looked around at the enthusiastic gathering. "There's just one thing I'd like to know," he said testily. "Who pushed me?"

It should not be too difficult for the intelligent man to understand why he needs to be prodded. Both psychology and Scripture agree— man needs a push and a pusher.

Psychology (the science of human behavior) reminds us of the negative factors fixed within us, stored away somewhere within the twelve billion cells of the brain. Man has been taught "you can't," "you must not," and "someone else can do it better than you," until something of the basic push God implanted within has departed. This is not to say that all of the negatives we were taught while young have been necessarily bad. In fact, some of them have been startlingly good. But now man needs a Bible—textbook direction as to what is good for him and what is not.

The average parent teaches in four ways—by his habits (which are not always good), by his words (not always wholesome), by his temperament (sometimes explosive), and by the whim of the moment!

"Friends" have done their share of feeding false information into the brain also. Boyce Evans was a traveling evangelist when I heard him speak. His subject that day—"Why Worry?" The message stressed proper mental attitude and suggested, "Man is primarily the sum total of his thoughts." He shared an illustration from his seminary days.

Three ministerial students decided to use a friend as a guinea pig to test whether a man's physical makeup could be changed by his mental attitude. Their "victim" pastored a small country church each weekend, and they set their trap when he returned to school at the start of the week.

"Didn't you sleep well last night?" the first friend asked, as the victim came whistling up the walk.

"Sure," he replied, and went on in.

A second man was stationed at the turn of the stairs. He started walking up the stairs with the pastor, and asked, "Bob, are you having trouble in your church?" Bob replied, "Well, I don't think so! At least not much."

The third man was stationed in the rear of the classroom. When Bob came in and took his seat, the third friend came over and said, "Friend, I am not a psychiatrist, but I can listen and if there is something you need to talk about, I would be glad to listen and try to help."

A bit of gloom settled over the victim's face. He answered, "Thank you, but I believe I can work it out." About forty-five minutes later he left class, whispering to one of the friends, "I'm going home. I'm sick."

Man is going to be motivated—the only question is how.

Kinds of Motivation

That which seeks to motivate from without is not real, lasting motivation. Psychology tells us that man has basic organic drives— drives which must be satisfied. Drives such as hunger and thirst, activity, rest, sex, physical labor, the body craving for a certain temperature range. These all fall into this physiological category.

Self-satisfaction of these drives is important. And if God instilled these drives, He apparently intended they would find their outlet. But in every case, He either built in saturation points or else gave specific governing rules. It is interesting that if there was not a Bible (our guidebook with specific direction as to how to act and what to do), man would have to invent one. So God gave us one—with wisdom straight from the storehouse of His knowledge—and all for our good.

The Chase

Aside from the physiological needs, man also has psychological needs. He longs for accomplishment of tasks and achievement of goals. Fundamental to his makeup is a desire to achieve. Even the infant in the crib expresses satisfaction when he has achieved.

At this point we need to be reminded that behavior is caused. "A stimulus leads to some sort of inter-action with an organism which is followed by behavior that we call a response. This response is also fed back to the organism as a stimulus."[1]

Man is going to be motivated—the only question is how.

The SOR (stimulus-organism-response) idea continually sends us searching for the right stimulus to motivate man. Consider a business corporation seeking to motivate an employee. What approach would be used?

To motivate an employee, a corporation may use fear.
Industry must lay down the rules of a job and rules invariably imply fear! A job description is placed in a man's hand. He is told, "This is the job to be done." The implication is that if the job assignment is not met, the person is fired. This type of reality therapy has him "living under the hammer." He works, he gives the desired response, but as time goes on something additional is needed.

Industry may also hope to stimulate the employee through the hope of future reward.
Reward (long-term benefits, salary raise, or both) is great—for a while. But let a blue Monday come, when the employee is coming apart at the seams, and the hope of reward, whether given at age sixty-five or in tomorrow's paycheck, seems to make no difference. He slows down in his work and unless something additional happens, he may well walk off the job—unmotivated.

Real motivation is motivation of the spirit.

When a man is motivated (moved toward action) from within, he will far surpass any achievements he would otherwise have accomplished, which brings us back exactly to what Mr. Webster was saying in his definitions. Prompting toward an action needs to work from the inside out.

Paul J. Meyer, founder of Success Motivation Institute, stated; "No matter who you are or what your age may be, if you want to achieve permanent, sustaining success, the motivation that will drive you toward that goal must come from within. It must be personal, deep-rooted and a part of your inner-most thoughts. All other motivation, the excitement of a crowd, the stimulation of a pep-talk, the exhilaration of a passing circumstance is external and temporary. It will not last."

Henry Ward Beecher suggested, "God made man to go by motives and he will not go without them, any more than a boat without steam, or a balloon without gas." Mack Douglas added, "Find what motivates men and we can touch the button; we can turn the key that makes men achieve miracles."

Back to the example of the factory worker. When the employer shared the job description and suggested they would be thrilled to have him as an employee, but only so long as he carried out the requirements, the employer was using motivation by fear. Was it wrong for him to do it? Not at all. Some would call it fear motivation, but an even better definition would be fact motivation. He would do the job, or he would be fired, and sharing the truth is a help, not a hindrance. The employee should forever be grateful the facts were shared (and the implications of dismissal) at the time of hiring—rather than not know about his job expectations and discover them later after he was fired.

Fear motivation in relation to accomplishment is not wrong, provided it is based on fact.

Is there anything wrong with reward motivation? Of course not. Again the same requirement must be met—the hope of reward must be based on fact. Reward motivation (offer of raise in salary or advancement in position) is absolutely wrong, even if it gets more work out of the man, if the employer cannot produce the reward.

Motivation of the spirit (attitude motivation) is, however, the best kind of motivation and cannot be surpassed by any other. SOR (stimulation-organism-response) has been set in motion but this time the response is a response from love. There is a "want-to" that's been changed on the inside. A man is motivated to work harder, achieve more, because his heart is in the company! And what employer isn't searching for that in his workers!

"How do you change a man on the inside?" becomes the question. What kind of power can re-make man? What is there that causes him to love the assembly line in spite of the fact it is boring and repetitious? Only a motivation of the spirit. When that has happened, a man is impelled to respond, whether or not circumstances are favorable.

Motivation by Application of the Bible

The secret to real motivation has been in the Bible for centuries. Not only does the Bible teach that man must be spurred to action from the inside, but God even sends His Holy Spirit to dwell within and provide the motivation. The same is true whether we speak of the physiological needs or the psychological.

God's help in the physiological area is twofold: first, He lays down laws which make for man's ultimate happiness; second, He thrusts His power within, enabling man to be able to keep those laws.

In the psychological area, the story of motivation is the same. As the power of God resides in the life through the Holy Spirit, man is motivated to accomplishment. The one who daily reads God's Word, and daily applies the "Three C's" (Chapter 15) discovers fantastic inner motivation.

In summary, the Bible attempts to direct man in some stunning principles of achievement. Too often we have considered that the Bible teaches nothing about success and accomplishment of goals. When, in fact, if we heed its commands, we will discover every command was for a purpose.

Principles of Achievement

1. Man is meant to achieve. Immediately after creation, man was told to be fruitful, multiply, replenish the earth, and subdue it.

2. Man must be motivated to achieve. Satan has many ways of implanting negatives in the mind, and the path of least resistance is the most well-trodden path.

3. Inner change is the beginning of the motivation process. Jesus designed the inner change idea. "Being converted and becoming as little children" and being "born again" was His idea. Paul said to the Corinthians, "Therefore if any man is in Christ, he is a new creature; the old things passed away, behold new things have come." Salvation is when we are "created in Christ Jesus for good works" (Eph. 2:10).

4. Motivation must be through daily repetition, feeding the brain with habits, thought patterns, and desires. "Pray without ceasing" and "rejoice in the Lord always" are not idle commands. The psalmist and Daniel each had daily habits of prayer, men in Berea examined the Scriptures daily (Acts 17:11), and the disciples went about sharing Christ with others on a daily basis (Acts 5:42). Repetition is essential in motivation.

5. Goal-setting is the necessary pointer to keep man moving in the right direction. From the time Jesus began His public ministry He seemed to have His goals set—He would please God, defeat the Devil, and die for the sins of man. Six months prior to Calvary, He stated that He "must go to Jerusalem, and suffer . . . and be killed, and be raised up on the third day" (Matt. 16:21). Earlier He had stated that the goal of His ministry was "to seek and to save that which was lost" (Luke 19:10).

6. Belief in God's power to accomplish His will through you is a must. Napoleon Hill said, "Whatever the mind of man can believe, it can achieve." Jesus said, "With God all things are possible" (Matt. 19:26). And again He said, "If you can! All things are possible to him who believes" (Mark 9:23).

19

MOTIVATION—EVEN IN TIMES OF SUFFERING

I am filled with comfort, I am exceeding joyful in all our tribulation.
—The Apostle Paul [1]

There wouldn't be a brook without rocks.
—S. M. Lockridge

Consider Jesus. He had one heavy cross to bear but He fixed His sight on the joy before Him. And we are to do the same.
—Joni Eareckson Tada [2]

A cartoon showed a man and a woman at a counter marked "Educational Toys." A clerk was showing them a box filled with odd-shaped fragments. "It's designed to prepare children for today's complex world. No matter how they put it together, it doesn't come out right."

Right at this point someone might plead, "Is this book going to be like some others I've read? Don't just talk about the good. What about my suffering? Nothing in life's puzzle makes sense to me due to my difficulties. Where does that fit in?"

"You see, I can believe God is interested in my success when my definition fits His. I can believe He is interested in helping me achieve goals He helps me set. But why my pain? I'm His! If God wants me to live on the mountaintop, to possess an inner thrill and radiance, to be surrounded by joy and peace, then I should have no suffering. Right?" Wrong.

143

The Chase

Suffering definitely relates to success and motivation. But not in the way the average man thinks.

Life Without Pain?

If you could have one wish, what would it be? High on the list of answers received to such a question would be, "Just give me life without pain." Most of us would agree, that would be good—but would it?

Little Beverly Smith, born in Akron, Ohio, almost never cried. She never cried when she fell down; she never cried when she bumped her head; she didn't even cry when she burned her hand on a hot stove. She cried only when she was hungry or angry.

The doctors soon discovered that she had a defect in the central nervous system for which no cure is known. She could not feel pain. The doctors told the mother she must watch Beverly constantly; the baby might break a bone and continue using it until it could not be set properly; she might develop appendicitis without nature's usual warning of pain. Spanking her to make her more careful about hot stoves and knives would do her no good; she wouldn't feel it. Life without pain would be perpetually dangerous.[3]

Back to the question, "Would it be a good thing for you to have life without pain? Think about it—would you really want life without pain?

Jesus said, "In the world you will have tribulation." (John 16:33 NKJV) That's not the same as saying that you might have it. You positively will have it. Tribulation, trouble, pain, and perplexity is a very normal part of life.

Of all people, Christians are certainly not exempt. If any person came to Christ believing life would automatically be a bed of roses, he received quite a surprise! Years ago, one of the professors at a seminary used to tell his young ministerial students, "Boys, be kind to everybody.

Everybody's got problems."

A study of the life of the apostle Paul would indicate that he had more problems than most anyone! Acts 14:19, and 2 Cor. 11:23-27 reveal that on different occasions he was beaten with rods, shipwrecked, and one time left for dead. Instead of life being easy, life was tough. He then added more—he had been on frequent journeys, in dangers from rivers, dangers from robbers, dangers from his countrymen, dangers from the Gentiles, dangers in the city, dangers in the wilderness, dangers on the sea, and dangers among false brethren. He spoke of sleepless nights, times without food and water, and he suffered through cold and exposure. If God meant to exempt Christians from problems and suffering, He forgot to tell Paul about it! A life without pain is apparently not God's intention.

Joy in Spite of Circumstances

Furthermore, the Christian is commanded to be joyful. Instead of joy ceasing when trouble begins, joy can continue in the midst of and in spite of suffering.

Jesus began teaching this idea in New Testament times. As a part of His Sermon on the Mount, Jesus proposed, "Blessed are you when men cast insults at you, and persecute you, and shall say all kinds of evil against you falsely, on account of Me. Rejoice and be glad" (Matt. 5:11–12). In the last week before the cross, Jesus said, "In the world you will have tribulation, but be of good cheer, I have overcome the world" (John 16:33 NKJV).

From a Philippian jail cell, God inspired Paul to write, sharing not despondency, but thrill. "Finally, my brethren, rejoice in the Lord" (Phil. 3:1). "Rejoice in the Lord always; again I will say, Rejoice!" (4:4).

In other writings, the same theme is echoed. The situation or circumstance surrounding the writing seemed to make no difference— the command was still the same. "Rejoice always" (1 Thess. 5:16). "In everything give thanks: for this is God's will for you in Christ Jesus" (v. 18). "The fruit of the Spirit is love, joy, peace, patience . . . " (Gal. 5:22). John must have seen even more suffering than Paul. Scholars tell us John did his writing about A.D. 95 when the persecutions of Emperor Domitian were in full swing. Someone said that by then approximately 50 percent of the population of the Roman Empire may have been slaves. Slaves in the Roman world were not considered people (Greek: *personae*) but "things" (Greek: *res*). Yet John mentions the great fellowship and joy that believers can have with the Father and His Son Jesus Christ. Later he speaks of having "no greater joy than to see that his children are walking in the truth."⁴

Just imagine—using the word "joy" in those dark days! To inspire those words, God must believe the believers can have inner joy and inner motivation no matter what!

Joni Eareckson Tada has been an amazing example to thousands and maybe millions in our time. Paralyzed after a diving accident, she became yielded to God in such a way that He has mightily used her as a popular author, speaker, and motivator. Ron Blue said that in a conversation with her one day, she shared her thoughts on 2 Peter 3:8 about how with God, a thousand years can be like one day and one day can be like a thousand years. He writes, "I had always interpreted that to mean that since a day was like a thousand years, God was not anxious about schedules or timetables, He has all the time in the world! While I still believe this assessment to be true, Joni opened my eyes to the other side of the verse. Since a thousand years is like a day, Joni said, each day becomes incredibly important in that it can have the eternal impact of a thousand years!"⁵

The Anguish of Defeat

One type of suffering often overlooked in a discussion of the problem is the suffering caused by defeat. FAILURE has to be spelled with capital letters in all our vocabularies. Who hasn't suffered because of himself?

Paul did. Prior to his conversion he failed God in a number of ways. To say that he later hated himself for his previous actions would be a big understatement. But Paul believed in the thoroughness of God's forgiveness, and that belief gave Paul a brand new beginning.

In the matter of a saved person disappointing God, John Mark has to be one of two classic examples. Acts 13:13 gives the sad account of his starting on the first missionary journey, and then turning back. More than that, his action almost split a beautiful friendship between Barnabas and Paul. (Acts 15:36-40). But bounce, did he bounce! When Paul writes his last letter prior to death, he urges Timothy to bring Mark "for he is profitable to me for the ministry" (2 Tim. 4:11). In addition, God used Mark to write a book of the Bible!

Simon Peter denied Jesus, but Jesus forgave him. For Simon not to forgive himself would have compounded his sin. He learned to believe Jesus, accept His forgiveness, and the once-defeated Simon became the preacher of Pentecost, and God's leader in the thrilling events to follow.

When Satan has won one victory, some throw up the white flag of surrender and let him have the whole war! Not Simon Peter!

If Mark and Peter, and even Paul could forget "the things that are behind," so can you. Just don't forget them until you have confessed your sin to God and received His promised forgiveness and cleansing according to 1 John 1:9.

> *God's great men and women have always been people of concern. They have known joy as a state of the heart but have, at the same time, been brokenhearted over conditions around them.*

Tears and Brokenness

What about tears? If a person is successful in their character and their goals, does this mean they will never weep again?

Contrariwise, the successful person will be a concerned person. They will be concerned about the will of God, the walk of their friends, and the way the world is going. The more successful he or she is, the more concerned he or she will be! A person can weep and be joyful at the same time. Joy is a fixed state of the heart, whereas tears are a God-given emotional outlet. One may be joyful over a thousand blessings God has given, plus joyful and excited about being a Christian, but when he stands in the presence of God he may well become broken.

Pity the poor person who thinks he is so successful he cannot show concern. He is not successful—he is proud, haughty, calloused, self-righteous, and blind to human need.

God's great men and women have always been people of concern. They have known joy as a state of the heart but have, at the same time, been brokenhearted over conditions around them.

David wept over his son Absalom. Jeremiah wept over a nation. Jesus wept over Jerusalem. Paul shed many tears in Ephesus over a space of three years. God's promise to the concerned soul-winner is, "He who continually goes forth weeping, bearing seed for sowing, shall doubtless come again with rejoicing, bringing his sheaves with him" (Psalm 126:6 NKJV).

Fullness of joy will never be discovered by one who runs from human need. God will resist the proud, but give grace to the humble! (Jas. 4:6; 1 Pet. 5:5).

The Big Jobs

God is on the lookout for people He can trust with giant problems. Giant tasks are everywhere in this world. There is, however, a prerequisite before you can be chosen for this job. Allow an explanation.

I read that when the construction of the Lockheed L-1011 airplane was completed, the company then began 18 months of rigorous testing, costing $1.5 billion dollars. Then the plane was put on their torture rack. It bends, twists, and pulls the structure of the plane to simulate the roughest treatment it will encounter in commercial operation.

Hydraulic jacks, electronic sensors, and a computer put the airplane through a fatigue test for a minimum of 36,000 flights. A lower wind joint of the jetliner underwent five lifetimes of simulated flight without failure, amounting to more than a hundred years of airline service.

Thirty-one 250-gallon water tanks were placed inside the test aircraft. The water tanks are connected by a series of pipes and pumps for transferring the aircraft's center of gravity in flight. Flight tests showed that the aircraft could handle a wider range of gravity than predicted by designers.

The plane was flown into ice clouds by test pilots. They wanted to check the operation of the anti-ice systems and see how the aircraft would respond to ice accretion. The flight test crew permitted heavy chunks of ice to break away from the nose of the aircraft and enter the rear mounted engine. They permitted heavy ice build-ups on one wing while keeping the other ice-free.[6]

That plane has been through it! I wouldn't mind flying on it, would you? Life is sometimes like that, and the testing times are no less easy.

But wouldn't it be just like God to take one look at the totally yielded Christian who had walked through sufferings and tensions, take another look at a giant task which desperately needed doing, then cast His eye back toward the Christian and write across his life—tested; trustworthy; yielded; motivated from within; ready for the big job!

PART SIX:

**Excitement Plus – The Result
Of Proper Motivation**

20

EXCITEMENT PLUS IN CHRISTIANITY

God has given us two hands—one to receive with and the other to give with. We are not cisterns made for hoarding; we are channels made for sharing.
—Billy Graham [1]

God has put Christ in us, the Bible says. Then it takes little or no imagination to believe that God has put in us the ability to do anything He wants done through us.
—whc

Motivation leads to excitement. Find the person who has a daily motivation of the Spirit, and you will find an excited person.

"I will not forget," Dr. Bill Bright stated, "as a young Christian, I read from a famous New Testament scholar, Dr. James Stewart of Edinburgh. I memorized what he said, it moved me so much. He said, 'If we could but show the world that being committed to Christ is no tame humdrum, sheltered monotony, but the most thrilling, exciting adventure the human spirit could ever know!'" Daily inner motivation by God's Spirit results in excitement plus!

When Dr. Robert Naylor was president of Southwestern Baptist Seminary, he was a featured preacher at one of the youth weeks at Falls Creek Baptist Encampment near Davis, Oklahoma. Preaching to the 7,000 youth and sponsors in attendance that week, he used a theme, "What Do You Think of Jesus?" When he came to the last night, he began his message with the words, "I've been asking you all week what you think of Jesus. I want to tell you what I think of Him. I just can't wait to walk the next mile with Him." Excitement plus!

153

> *Motivation leads to excitement. Find the person who has a daily motivation of the Spirit, and you will find an excited person.*

Spiritually hungry, a nightclub entertainer drifted into a revival meeting in Alabama. When the service had concluded, she shared with the pastor, "This is the most unique and exciting thing I have ever seen in my life."

Christianity has always been that way. It was born in the heart of God with the intention of being an exciting, thrilling, and heaven-sent answer to the needs of man.

Our generation shall give an account to God if we have lacked enthusiasm. Someone sadly commented that modern preachers have been able to do what no one has been able to do for 2,000 years—make Christ appear dull. If that is true of any preacher, it is unbelievably tragic. The watermark our generation must leave behind was rightly stated by Dr. Stewart—"Christianity is the most thrilling, exciting adventure the human spirit could ever know."

Sources of Excitement

Being convinced that God wants us to be happy, motivated, and excited about life, the question arises, "How?" Already we have noted that true motivation has to come from within. Excitement is similar. It cannot be faked. False excitement ruins character. Honest excitement builds character. There are six basic sources of excitement:

1. The excitement of being needed
2. The excitement of being usable
3. The excitement of being on the winning team
4. The excitement of the "greater-than" concept
5. The excitement of expectation (faith)

6. The excitement of goal-setting and goal-reaching

Now for our study of excitement. These sources could well be memorized. They bear oft-repeating.

1. Excitement comes from being needed.

Consider the person who has been defeated. He imagines he is not needed. He believes the Devil's lie. Wise was the man who said, "It makes no difference who you are or what you are, or how discouraged you may be, if you are still alive, God has a purpose for your life."

James McConkey, whose 1918 writing of The Three-Fold Secret of the Holy Spirit remains a classic, has another work entitled, The Surrendered Life. In this work McConkey wrote about the pulls that come upon a young person's life.

> The Lord hath need of thee, saved one. Trade, with all its rush, and fever, and wear, and waste, lays its hands upon the Christian and says curtly: "I need you to plan, think, toil, accumulate, and die in my service." Society, too, asserts its claim, and says: "I need you with your wit, beauty, talents and accomplishments to shine in the brilliant circles of fashion, and will give you pleasure without limit if you will yield to me." Professional life lays its hand on him and says: "I need you to adorn your chosen calling, and will gratify your highest ambitions if you will come." But there comes a voice, softly floating down twenty vanished centuries, a voice which whispers to every redeemed child of God in the hour when wealth, and pleasure, and ambition have failed to satisfy his secret longings; a voice which is true today as of old: "The Lord hath need of thee."[2]

There are so many people in the world to be helped, and each of us can be used to help others. In China alone, there are 1.3 billion people and if those were lined up four abreast to begin marching around the world, the line would never come to an end. In Jesus' day there were 250 million people in the world; in A.D. 1600, 500 million; in A.D. 1900, 1.5 billion; jumping to 6 billion in the year 2000, and in July 2012 the world population was estimated to be nearly 7 billion.

When a philosopher found himself in a concentration camp, he spent several years watching his friends struggle to stay alive. He concluded, "He who has a *why* to live can live with almost any how."

Your *why* is that Christ needs you. Christ needs you in a world where people are falling apart. God, in His mighty plan, thrust you into the most exciting and troubled generation ever. There are people you can reach no one else can ever reach. The Lord hath need of thee!

2.   Excitement comes from being usable.

The thrilling life is the usable life. The first-century disciples also gained a great deal of excitement because they knew they were usable. They stayed on their knees until they were. Then they expected God to use them.

In our honest moments we know God cannot use an unclean vessel. When sin is confessed, and the vessel is clean, the individual is usable. Paul tells Timothy that "if a man cleanses himself…, he will be a vessel for honor, sanctified, useful to the Master, prepared for every good work" (2 Tim. 2:21). Just as sin in the life removes every trace of excitement, confession and cleansing can restore it.

Someone recently gave me an outline entitled "The Man God Uses." The list is excellent for periodic checkup.

THE MAN GOD USES

1.   He has but one great purpose in life.
2.   He has, by God's grace, removed every hindrance from his life.

3. He has placed himself absolutely at God's disposal.
4. He has learned how to prevail in prayer.
5. He is a student of the Word.
6. He has a vital, living message for the lost world.
7. He is a man of faith who expects results.
8. He works in the anointing of the Holy Spirit.

Some years ago, two missionaries in China were talking. One was praying, "Lord, use me." The other said, "Stop praying like that. It's not any of your business whether the Lord uses you or not. You just get usable."

Vance Havner remarks, "Stop praying, 'Lord, use me' and get usable and the Lord will wear you out!"

3. Excitement comes from the "winning team concept."

Attend a football game and watch the crowd. At the outset everybody is excited. But soon excitement grows or lags depending on whose team is winning.

The resurrection of Christ turned eleven disheartened disciples around. They had previously *thought* they were on the winning team, but when even the grave could not hold Christ, they *knew* they were on the winning team! And their excitement grew by the moment. "With boldness" (Acts 4:31), "with great power" (4:33), "full of grace and power" (6:8), and "continually filled with joy" (13:52) became common descriptive terms in the book of Acts. Some even said they were turning the world upside down—actually they were turning it right-side up! They were excited and had reason to be—they were on the winning team.

Consider the book of Revelation. Written in one of the dark hours of persecution, the theme is "Get excited—we're on the winning team!"

4. Excitement comes from the "greater-than" concept.

Another thought that leaps from the lives of the first-century disciples is the "greater-than" concept. How could a few men (fishermen, tax collectors, common laborers, and the like) be charged with enough enthusiasm to take on the first-century Roman world? They believed (1) Christ lived in them and (2) Christ was greater-than . . .! They went about thinking, "Greater is He who is in you, than he who is in the world" (1 John 4:4). Christ had given them an advanced preview of that thought in His last conversation with them (John 14:17–23).

The promises of God are not all past or future tense. Check them out for the here-and-now:

"The Lord is the defense of my life" (Ps. 27:1).

"Thanks be to God, who gives us the victory through our Lord Jesus Christ" (1 Cor. 15:57).

"We overwhelmingly conquer through him that loved us" (Rom. 8:37).

"My grace is sufficient for you" (2 Cor. 12:9).

"[Our God] is able to do exceeding abundantly beyond all that we ask or think" (Eph. 3:20).

"The Lord is my shepherd" (Ps. 23:1).

"There is therefore now no condemnation for those who are in Christ Jesus" (Rom. 8:1).

"God is able to make all grace abound to you" (2 Cor. 9:8).

"Greater is he who is in you, than he who is in the world" (1 John 4:4).

5. Excitement comes from expectation (faith).

These are all present tense promises—not past tense, not future tense, but present tense promises. That's exciting!

Jim Hylton excitingly comments, "You can't write checks on the

158

Bank of Heaven until you know your account. But once you know what kind of account you have in heaven, you can go and start writing checks on it (on your privileges). But if you don't know what kind of account you have, you are not going to be drawing on the resources of God."

Imagine waking up each morning, thinking, "I can draw on the resources of God!" Of course you can—if your account is right and up-to-date.

The person God will choose to use will be the one who has faith and expects results. God is insulted by those who hold a "little God" concept, yet the biggest thing millions ask Him to do each day is "bless the food."

Henry Ford said, "Whether or not you think you can, you're right!" I would add, "Whether or not you think God can do it through you, you're right!" If you refuse to honor God enough to believe Him for big things, He will go on only blessing your food.

If a man refuses to believe God for big things, let him at least not blame God when nothing happens. Let him wonder no longer why excitement never comes his way—excitement comes from expectation.

6.   **Excitement comes from goal-setting and goal-reaching.**

Not failure, but low aim, is our crime. Perhaps the subject of goals demands a study all by itself. We'll tackle that in the next chapter.

Christ in You

You've just learned six good sources of excitement. Don't forget them. Could we summarize all six statements by saying—You have every right to be excited if Christ is in your life. "Christ in you, the hope of glory!" (Col. 1:27). Jesus Christ is the—

The Chase

Source of your being needed,
 Reason you can be usable,
  Coach of the winning team,
   Secret to the "greater-than" concept,
    Author of your expectation
     Power in goal-setting and goal-
     reaching.

Stay close to the Source and you'll get excited. Follow Jesus from afar and you'll drift into a dull, routine-like existence. You don't want to exist; you want to live. You don't want to just think excitement, you want to live excitement.

Every saved person can rejoice and say—"Christ in me! I just can't wait to walk the next mile with Him!"

21

GOAL-SETTING AND GOD

There came a time in my life when I earnestly prayed: "God, I want Your power!" Time wore on and the power did not come. One day the burden was more than I could bear. "God, why haven't You answered that prayer?" God seemed to whisper back His simple reply. "With plans no bigger than yours, you don't need My power."
—Carl Bates

One thing I do, forgetting what lies behind and reaching forward to what lies ahead, I press on toward the goal for the prize of the upward call of God in Christ Jesus.
—Goal of the apostle Paul

Some years ago a headline told of 300 whales which suddenly died. The whales were pursuing sardines and found themselves marooned in a bay. Frederick Brown Harris commented, "The small fish lured the sea giants to their death . . . . They came to their violent demise by chasing small ends, by prostituting vast powers for insignificant goals."

What kinds of goals do you have? Answer that question honestly for me, and I can tell you how much excitement you have in your life.

Christians, of all people, need to wrestle with the concept of goals. Sharon Ramsey says, "To me, having the vision of success means having goals and knowing how to achieve them. Having a road map for your goals is a beginning. You need to set limits on what you want to accomplish within your lifestyle. Occasionally, I have to say no to some projects, because if my platter gets too full, I'm not going to do a good job at the most important things. Goals and visions cannot be reached if you are torn in a million different directions."[1]

The Chase

I know what she is talking about, because there was an earlier time in my life when I would have had trouble being specific about goals. I am thankful it was sometime later when a salesman came by my office to talk with me about success. In the course of his sales speech, he asked me to take a sheet of paper and a pen, and write down three big goals in my life. He said he would time me with his watch, and I would have 60 seconds to do it. I did it within one minute, but I would have been embarrassed had he appeared on the scene a few years before that. As Christians, when we set no goals, we usually reach all we have!

Problems of Goal-Setting

"But I have problems with this thing of goal-setting!" several voices quickly say. Relax. Probably everyone either has a problem or once had a problem. But what's yours?

Problem No. 1 in Goal-setting: The problem of finding the correct concept of Christian contentment.

Dedicated Darla inquires, "Do you want to know my problem in setting goals? I read the Bible quite a bit and consider myself fairly knowledgeable. I can give you three reasons as to why I've hesitated to set goals. My reasons are all Scripture verses."

"Be content with what you have" (Heb. 13:5).

"I have learned to be content in whatever circumstances I am" (Phil. 4:11).

"But godliness actually is a means of great gain, when accompanied by contentment" (1 Tim. 6:6).

Rather difficult to argue with the Scriptures, isn't it? "So that means I should set no goals, right?" Darla ponders her own question.

Hm-m-m. Let's study Darla's situation. She is absolutely right in her desire to obey God's Word. The Bible was written to provide wonderful instruction and one good rule Darla has learned is to always obey God's Word. She has also learned that every rule God has given is, in reality, for her own good. Her mistake is in interpretation. Contentment does not mean what Darla has interpreted it to mean. Hence, her error of setting no goals.

Those who wrestle with the meaning of contentment could come up with two possibilities. So how about a multiple choice test. Which of the two would you circle as being correct?

The meaning of contentment is: (circle the correct one)

1. I should have my desires limited to that which I already have, and that which I have already achieved.
2. I should have my desires limited to that which I am convinced God wants me to have, and that which God wants me to achieve.

There's a world of difference in those two ideas of contentment! The first spells laziness; the second spells lordship! Christian contentment majors on the lordship of Christ. Lordship (having Christ in the control tower) should be the primary prerogative in the study of every Christian concept.

The Christian should decide that whatever he does in the area of setting goals or not setting goals, he will do under the lordship of Christ. You can stake your life on the fact that however God meant for us to interpret those verses, the outcome would not belittle the lordship of Christ. Everything a Christian does must center around having Christ in the control tower.

If Christ is in the control tower, what will my Christian contentment mean? Contentment must not be interpreted as laziness, indifference, unconcern, apathy, prayerlessness, or failure to witness, because godliness and contentment are to be a part of the same life. However, there is a concept which will not belittle the meaning of contentment, or do away with godliness, or take Christ's prerogatives as Lord of the life. Allow me to submit what I believe was Paul's concept of Christian contentment.

1. I am thrilled today with what God has given me. I am wonderfully satisfied.

2. My thrill today is by no means a guarantee that God intends I be thrilled tomorrow with the same things.

3. I want my desires limited (if need be) to that which God wants me to have, and that which God wants me to achieve.

4. I also want my desires stretched (if need be) to that which I am convinced God wants me to have, and that which God wants me to achieve.

There's a picture of contentment under the lordship of Christ. Whether the desires will need to be limited or stretched will be a matter of daily wisdom that is achieved in time alone with God.

God may more often require a stretching rather than a shrinking! In fact, He rebukes us for our failure to stretch, for not thinking big. "You do not have because you do not ask!" (James 4:2 NASB).

Goal-setting for the Christian is simply planned, organized, stretching under the lordship of Christ.

Problem No. 2 in Goal-Setting: The problem of previous defeat.

Defeated Dan has a different kind of problem. He doesn't mind setting goals—he just has never reached any goal.

As a result, the defeat and despair he feels within results in a downcast spirit in everything he does. It even shows on his face.

Defeated Dan does have a problem—a very real problem.

Dr. Clyde M. Narramore spent years as a consultant in research and guidance for the schools of Los Angeles County. Then he became founder of the Rosemead School of Psychology. He shares his pertinent words:

> It's not easy to be enthusiastic about the future when one has not been successful in the past. Failure dims our outlook. Tomorrows seldom look bright if our yesterdays have been marred by dissatisfaction . . . . There's nothing like failure to kill incentive and ambition. People don't mind working hard when the reward is accomplishment. But to work without results is no better than aimlessly marking time— going 'round and 'round in the same old rut, getting nowhere. It's like a donkey on a treadmill. And that's when life becomes the "same old grind."[2]

Yes, it takes more than striving to develop a well-adjusted personality. It also takes some arriving. Should the defeated person be advised to never again set goals? Or is the problem not with goal-setting but with improper goal-setting?

The goals Dan chose were too big, unattainable. Not reaching any of the goals, he soon felt he couldn't do what others do. "I'm just a natural-born failure," he said to himself.

Parents who are perfectionists may have led to such a condition. Parental goals may always have been so big, so unattainable, that Dan felt he was never able to "just enjoy being me, for Jesus' sake."

Or Dan may have been overly ambitious. Not praying about his goals, maybe he chose some out of pure selfishness. "I'll show them who I am and what I can do." God just could not bless that. Result—a defeated person.

The defeated and downcast person should first go to his knees in prayer. Let him lay down all his previous goals, surrendering them to the lordship of Christ. He should confess his sin of trying to "heap riches unto himself" (if that was his sin), or the sin of forgetting to use the head God gave him, or blundering by setting what should have been a yearly goal as his monthly goal.

Let him set a goal for something he knows he can attain this week— he will have to stretch a bit—yes, but a goal he knows he can attain. At

165

week's end, to use Dr. Narramore's words, he will not be *striving* but *arriving*. Next week his goal can be a bit bigger, but let him not bite off impossible chunks and develop "give-up-i-tis."

Problem No. 3 in Goal-Setting: The problem of fuzziness in the financial area.

Read a dozen books on goal-setting and you'll understand the problem *Moneymad Merle* developed. Half of the books convinced him that anyone who would buy the book and apply the rules should soon be a millionaire. Merle didn't make it! He even began to blame God for lousing him up! After all, some guys were making it.

The question comes as to whether God is interested in Merle's finances. Let's switch from Merle to you. You may wonder if God is interested in your finances. Certainly.

How do you know? God is interested in *you*! You have to spend a lot of time thinking about finances. If you believed in worry, you would spend a lot of time worrying about them. In other words, they are your concern. God urges you to cast "all your care [concern] upon him; for he cares for you" (1 Pet. 5:7). To care about your concerns, God would have to care about your finances.

God is probably not at all interested in making you a millionaire. Eight of ten millionaires may have no time for God—just time for money. In other words, money ruins their sense of values. It's a rare man who is not ruined by a lot of money. God is not interested in ruining a man's values, or home relationships, or giving him a big head, or in making him spend all his time figuring out how to make more. God has helped a few men become millionaires, knowing their millions could be used for His glory. But interested in ruining a man? Not God.

Of course, neither does God want His children to be always looking as if God cannot properly provide for them. Believers should be good advertisements for God, not bad ones. The God who owns the cattle on a thousand hills will care for His own. He always provides, but whether we spend what we have correctly is another matter.

There is a vast difference between needs and wants. The promise of God is that He will supply your needs (Phil. 4:19). Many a person has gotten in serious financial trouble because God supplied enough for his needs, but the individual used it to satisfy his wants.

Need financial advice? God's success book suggests that we (1) Put God first in our lives, not "things" (Matt. 6:33); (2) Believe God for His help in meeting our needs (Phil. 4:19); (3) Pray about even the smallest matter of concern (Phil. 4:6; 1 Pet. 5:7); (4) Pay debts promptly (Prov. 3:28); (5) Give God at least one tenth of our income (Mal. 3:8–10); (6) Avoid surety, or the guaranteeing of another's note (Prov. 11:15; 17:18; 22:26); (7) Refuse to love money (1 Tim. 6:10;) (8) Work for our income (Ex. 20:9; 2 Thess. 3:10).

Should a person think of setting goals in the financial area? That depends—will God or the individual get the glory from attainment? Will the lives of others be wonderfully blessed if you are blessed? Will people be reached for Christ because of your blessing? It is not wrong to have material goals—just make sure God is the one who gives them to you rather than you giving them to God. Basically, we are all tempted to be selfish.

Pray about your financial situation. Ask God about your goals. After all, He's the captain in charge and He would not want you to have anything which could later hurt you.

Problem No. 4 in Goal-Setting: The problem of paralyzing mediocrity.

Now for the biggest problem of all. More problems develop in the goal-setting area over this one hang-up than over all the rest. Whereas *Defeated Dan* had harmed himself with setting goals too big, *Easygoing Ernest* sets goals so small they are dishonoring and displeasing to the

The Chase

God who made him. But the worst case scenario may be *Lazy Larry*. His kind find it difficult to even want to be motivated.

PATIENT: "Tell me Doc, in plain English, just what's wrong with me."

DOC: "You're just plain lazy."

PATIENT: "Doc, could you give me a long, hard-to-pronounce medical term for that condition, so I could use it when I tell my friends?"

There is no excuse for laziness, apathy, or indifference in a believer's life. A majority of those who have no goals may be guilty of paralyzing mediocrity.

Goals and God's Giants

People who have power with God are not afraid of goals. They thrive on them. God apparently has no fear of them—He assigns them.

Abraham's goal was to follow God anywhere, to the end of the earth if necessary, and gather people around him who would walk by faith. Moses' goal was to rescue all the Jews from bondage and lead them toward the Promised Land. David's goal was to save his people from the Philistines, even if he had to fight Goliath himself. Elijah's goal was to destroy Baal worship in Israel. No risk was too great, no odds too big. Elisha's goal was to have a double portion of the spirit and power of Elijah resting upon him, and he would not be denied. Christ's goal—He stated it in two ways—"For the Son of man has come to seek and to save that which was lost" (Luke 19:10), and "I came that they might have life, and might have it more abundantly" (John 10:10).

A person without goals comes to the end of life only to discover that the bulk of their life history can be summarized by:

20 years of sleeping

5 years of dressing and personal care

3 years of waiting on others

2 years on social media

4 months of tying his shoes, and

6 years of watching television.

Without goals the routines of life become the ruts of life!

Even books of the Bible have goals. When God inspired John to write several books of the Bible, the goal was established. "These have been written, that you may believe that Jesus is the Christ, the Son of God, and that believing you may have life in His name" (John 20:31). When 1 John was penned, a twofold goal was shared: "These things we write, so that our joy may be made complete" (1 John 1:4); and "These things I have written to you…in order that you may know that you have eternal life" (1 John 5:13).

Second John (v.12) again shares God's goal to the recipients: "Having many things to write to you, I would not write with paper and ink; but I hope to come to you and speak face to face; that your joy may be made full!" The goal of 3 John is, "Beloved, I pray that in all respects you may prosper and be in good health, just as your soul prospers"(v.2). The importance of goals is underlined by Dr. Howard G. Hendricks. "I have never met a Christian who sat down and planned to live a mediocre life. But if you keep going in the direction in which you are moving, you may land there."[3]

Test Your Goals

It is not enough to have goals, the Christian should also test them. Here is a "Christian's Check List for Testing Goals."

1. Do all my goals fit into the context of my written, stated purpose for my life (life-long goal)?
2. Have I been honest enough to set goals in every area of life, believing God is interested in the total "me"—spiritual area? recreational area? professional area? social area? educational and intellectual area? family relationship

    area? financial area?

3. Have I developed a plan of long-range, short-range, and immediate goals? Have I developed them in that order so the long-range goal will predetermine my other goals?

4. Can my goals glorify God or are they selfish in nature?

5. Did I ask God for His wisdom and guidance before I attempted to establish these goals?

6. Would Jesus Christ be willing to be Lord of my life and preside over the reaching of goals such as mine?

7. If I am thoroughly convinced these are God-given goals, then cannot I expect His power to work in the achievement of these goals?

A few years ago T. B. Maston shared some excellent tests and questions. Although he wrote them as a gauge by which a Christian could measure his activities, I have taken the liberty to add a word or two and suggest they can also apply to goals.

Three Questions:

    1. How will it affect me?

    2. How will it affect others?

    3. How will it affect the cause of Christ?

Three Tests:

    1. Test of secrecy—is it all right if others know my goals?

    2. Test of universality—would it be all right for everyone else to have these goals?

    3. Test of prayer—were my goals born in prayer?

Three Sources of Light:

    1. Light from within.

    2. Light from without (others).

    3. Light from above (God).[4]

The main goal of a Christian should not be to be a better Christian.

Too selfish. Jesus said we should bear fruit, not be better fruit. We will not be better fruit unless we bear fruit. When we are not interested in others, we become self-centered. When we try to save ourselves, we lose ourselves. Only as we lose ourselves in service to God, can we please Him. "He who is wise wins souls" (Prov. 11:30).

Even a church should test its goals! One pastor became aware his church had no goals. Then he became convicted that the fault was not with the members, but himself. He prayed over the matter and God gave him three statements which he then placed at the head of every job description. "The Philosophy of the Church," the pastor called it. Notice how goals are built into it.

1. The church is the biggest business in the world, not one of the biggest businesses, but the biggest. Therefore, the church should be the best run business in the world, running more efficiently than any other.

2. The church should be the most honest business in the world, never teaching that it is all right for a worker, paid or unpaid, to do less than his best.

3. The purpose of the church is twofold, according to the Great Commission of Christ: (1) to win people to Christ, and (2) to teach them to do all things which Christ commanded them to do.

People at the church now have goals in mind, and frequently speak of the exciting things God is doing.

Excitement is vitally related to goal-setting. And the excitement rapidly grows with goal reaching. Ready for a dare? First, I dare you to ask God to give you some goals. Second, I dare you to apply the "Christian's Check List for Testing goals"—apply it to your goals until you can answer all seven questions in the affirmative. Third, I dare you to put your goals under the scrutiny of T. B. Maston's "Three Questions, Three Tests, and Three Sources of Light." Fourth, I dare you to try to keep from getting excited when God's enabling power works through you and you begin to see your (really His) goals reached.

22

STRETCHING YOUR DREAMS!

> *God is a wonderful God who would love to help you grow and stretch. How? Toward bigger dreams, bigger goals! You can do more than you ever thought you could. How? "He is able to do exceeding abundantly beyond all that we ask or think."* [1] *If He sees that you are someone He can continually trust, then He can put His power in you and on you, and stretch you with His ability.*
> —whc

> *When the going gets tough, the tough get going.*
> —Motto from a football team's locker room.

Did you hear about the guy that wanted to be stretched? Newspaper accounts said that for years this man had wanted to be a policeman, but he was too short. He would not be defeated. He tried every kind of stretching exercise he could imagine. He even had his wife put a bump on his head (most wives don't charge for that!). He said he gained an inch and a half. I'm not sure he made the police requirements, but a guy with zeal like that is hard to beat!

Stretching exercises! Who would have ever thought of that? That's ingenuity!

Many Christians are in desperate need of stretching—mind stretching, spiritual mind stretching. We're in the biggest business or biggest mission in the world, so it is imperative that we think like big thinkers.

India—what did I learn? I was in a large city, speaking to a large crowd each evening, and leading a Pastor's Conference for some 40 or more pastors each morning. After one of the morning sessions, I was asked a question by one of the Indian pastors. "Dr. Cook, do you know what the problem is with American Christians?" All I could think to say was, "Tell me. What do you think is wrong with American Christians?" I can almost still hear his 4-word reply—"They think too small!"

Imagine being a small thinker in the world's biggest business!

I Dare You to Stretch

Satan is an expert in tempting us to withdraw into our little world and major on minors. Let the average Christian reach one other person for Christ in a year, and he is unbelievably content. If our minds were to begin to fathom the things God wants to accomplish through us, there would be no end to our excitement.

One day while thinking on my favorite verse, Ephesians 3:20, God hit me with an astounding thought-provoker. God seemed to say, "Don't you see the challenge I am giving you? You cannot out-ask Me; you cannot out-think Me; you cannot out-imagine Me; you cannot out-dream Me; you cannot out-do Me, for I am able to do exceeding abundantly beyond all that you ask or think."

Incredible! But there was God daring me to think—daring me to stretch my imagination to the farthest limits, and then telling me He could still go beyond that. And that wasn't all—in the same verse He showed the way He would do it "according to the power that works within us." Suddenly I saw it even clearer—God wanted to accomplish through us, according to the power He had already placed in us.

> *God has no third team. Everyone He saves is on His first team.*

Force Yourself to New Thinking

Anyone who walks with God very closely for very long is going to be involved in a constant stretching process. The stretching will always begin in the mind.

The beginning concept will be for the believer to learn that God has no little assignments. That which seems small is extremely big because it is from God.

Where is the employer who hires a person and starts them moving mountains overnight? Rather, the employer may start the new employee in a back room somewhere and watch him tackle that assignment. But that back room is one whale of a big assignment. If the trainee doesn't do that job right, he or she stays in the back room from now on. Many a Christian feels unwanted because he thinks he's on God's third team. God has no third team. Everyone He saves is on His first team. If God assigns what seems to be a small task, let that person remember the Employer is watching to see if he or she can do little things in a big way. Jesus said, "He who is faithful in a very little thing is faithful also in much." (Luke 16:10 NASB) God considers no assignment as a small one. He checks every job to see how it is done.

Another concept to quickly learn is that no one should ever wait for special assignments from God. You may already know the names of a few you might attempt to reach for Christ and salvation. Consider those as God-given assignments. Pray and expect God to place individuals in your path. Expect impressions and surprises! Pray often for those by name. Jesus said, "You shall be My witnesses!"[2] Don't expect God to trust you with some giant task if you haven't started on the sharing assignment He gave nearly 2,000 years ago.

You must also force yourself into exciting new thinking in the area of problems. God doesn't know a single problem He cannot turn into an opportunity. For centuries God has been taking what man considered as a problem and turning it into an opportunity—an opportunity for

175

The Chase

Him to work a miracle. When are we going to stretch our imaginations to realize that the fulfillment of dreams begins with the problems that are right around us? When will we see through the eyes of eternity and view problems as opportunities?

"But you don't know the size of my problem. If you did, you wouldn't consider it an opportunity." No, but God knows the size of it. And He has handled problems a lot bigger than that. Problems are but opportunities in work-clothes, stepping stones to even greater-sized victories.

Consider the greatest Christian you know. He or she has, no doubt, faced unbelievable obstacles all along the path. Long ago, however, that person learned the lesson of taking those things immediately to God—not to the worry closet! Do you wonder why that Christian possesses such peace?

"I have two things I can do with what appears to be a problem," the thrilled Christian says. "First, I can worry with it; second, I can trust it to God. If I worry, I am doubting God's ability to handle it. If I trust it to God, I have His promise that He will give me the right solution in His perfect timing (see Jas. 1:5–7)."

Blind Alleys Can Become Bold Challenges

When David met Goliath, the shepherd boy looked at the giant and exclaimed, "The battle is the Lord's!" That type of thinking can bring a new perspective to huge problems. What if each believer stood tall enough in his relation to God, that he could truly trust God in the tough hours. Think of it—in relation to those big concerns you have—the battle is the Lord's. Or to word it another way, the battle is the Lord's and the thrill of victory is ours! If your life is going to be stretched into the exciting life God wants it to be, you will be forced to always think of God as a big God able to meet big needs.

Dr. Donald Grey Barnhouse tells of the day he was invited back to Princeton Theological Seminary to preach to the students, after being away for twelve years. One of his former Hebrew professors came to sit on the front row of Miller Chapel. At the close of the meeting, the old gentleman came by to comment. He remarked that he always tried to come to Chapel when a former student was speaking for the first time. "When I hear them, I know what their ministry will be," he commented. "Some men have a little god, and they are always in trouble with him. He can't do any miracles. He can't take care of the inspiration and transmission of the Scripture to us. He doesn't intervene on behalf of his people. They have a little god. . .

Then some have a great God. He speaks and it is done. He commands and it stands fast. He knows how to show Himself strong on behalf of them that fear Him. You have a great God; and He will bless your ministry." Dr. Barnhouse said that old Dr. Wilson paused a moment, smiled and said, "God bless you," and walked out.[3]

God's stretching process frequently requires that we see blind alleys as bold challenges. There are two ways to view uncertainties—with fear and dread, or with the excitement of expectancy.

Practically no one wanted to go to Africa when C. T. Studd left England to go in 1910. They had no idea what was out there! Mr. Studd saw it as an exciting challenge. His biography preserves these thrilling words: "Some wish to live within the sound of Church or Chapel bell; I want to run a Rescue Shop, within a yard of hell." C. T.'s motto was: "If Jesus Christ be God, and died for me, then no sacrifice can be too great for me to make for Him."

Contrast Abraham with the Israelites who followed Moses. Abraham left Ur of the Chaldees, and "went out, not knowing where he was going" (Heb. 11:8). The thrill of the unknown led him to become one of God's greatest men ever.

Those who left Egypt with Moses, on the other hand, could not stand uncertainties. When they heard the majority report of the committee which spied out Canaan, they gave up. "How often they rebelled against him in the desert! And again and again they tempted God, and pained the Holy One of Israel" (Ps. 78:40-41). They returned to the wilderness to die, even when the people in Canaan had already given up (Josh. 2:9–11)!

What if??? *What if the Israelites had asked God to stretch them and stretch their dreams? They would have discovered that blind alleys can become bold challenges.* Think of some big uncertainty or some big problem facing you as you face tomorrow. Look at it this way—the uncertainties of each tomorrow can make exciting opportunities for a big God.

23

THE EXCITING ROLE OF FAITH

The pilgrims, then, especially Christian, began to de-
spond in his mind, and looked this way and that, but no
way could be found by which they might escape the river.
Then they asked the men if the waters were all of an equal
depth. "No," said they, "you shall find it deeper or shal-
lower as you believe in the King of the place."
—*John Bunyan*
Pilgrim's Progress

All things are possible to him that believeth.
—*Jesus Christ*

Faith is believing God. Someone has spoken of "the magic of believing." Faith is not magic but it works just that wonderfully. Faith is the one principle on the human side without which God will not move from the divine side.

What one word in the Bible separates the men from the boys? Faith. Why has God chosen to bless some of His people considerably more than others? Faith. What have the great achievers possessed in their makeup which most of us have missing from ours? Faith.

Faith, or the lack of it, is the stock-market barometer of our confidence. When our faith is right, we are right. We possess enthusiastic confidence, a God-given sense of expectancy, an inner peace which cannot be swayed by the circumstances of the moment.

Pick out the greatest Christian you know—and no doubt he excels in faith. Pick out the greatest Christian in Bible times—and faith was a dynamic he possessed.

Check your faith pulse. Are you satisfied with it? Has faith become a life-style for you?

Only when we believe do we begin to achieve.

Faith plays a giant part in success. If success is the continuing achievement of being the person God wants you to be, and the continuing achievement of established goals God helps you set, it is imperative to recognize the role of faith. In fact, we can ask God's guidance in giving us goals. We can write them on paper and read them aloud daily or once a week; we can even pray over them. But until we believe, nothing will happen. *Only when we believe do we begin to achieve.*

The Importance of Faith

Earlier in chapter 9, we noted the word "faith" is in the New Testament 246 times, and the word "believe" 136 times. Since "faith" and "believe" are from the exact same root in the original Greek (the only difference being in the verb or noun ending), then this one idea appears in the New Testament 382 times. This is astounding evidence that God places unusual importance as to where we stand in the arena of faith.

To read the New Testament record of Old Testament heroes is to again underline the emphasis of faith.

By *faith*, Abel   By *faith*, Abraham
By *faith*, Enoch   By *faith*, Joseph
By *faith*, Noah   By *faith*, Moses

are common expressions in the book of Hebrews, chapter 11. By faith the walls of Jericho fell, and through faith God's people have subdued kingdoms, performed acts of righteousness, obtained promises, and stopped the mouths of lions. And as if that is not enough, the writer names several more amazing things.

From the lips of Jesus came frequent expressions about faith. "And He said to them, If you have faith as a mustard seed . . . nothing shall be impossible to you" (Matt. 17:20). "Therefore I say to you, all things for which you pray and ask, believe that you have received them, and they shall be granted to you" (Mark 11:24). "And everything you ask in prayer, believing, you shall receive" (Matt. 21:22). "Jesus said unto him, All things are possible to him that believes" (Mark 9:23). "Be it done to you according to your faith" (Matt. 9:29).

From the other side, the Bible comments that "without faith it is impossible to please him" (Heb. 11:6). "This is the victory that overcomes the world—our faith" (1 John 5:4). God provides the power which enables Spirit-filled believers to accomplish the given task, but faith is the key which unlocks the power. Faith is operative regardless.

When everything about us seems downright bleak. . .
When the heart is broken almost beyond repair,
When others would point us in another direction,
When needs are so gigantic as to be unreal,
When it seems Satan's whole army is marching against us,
When an inner voice says, "What's the use?"
When the understanding is unbelievably weak,
Faith goes right on.

Things don't change faith. Faith changes things. And the power of God is called on the scene.

The Definition of Faith

Hebrews 11:1 is excellent for the definition of faith. Try checking the verse in the different versions.

King James Version—"Faith is the substance of things hoped for, the evidence of things not seen."

New American Standard Bible—"Now faith is the assurance of things hoped for, the conviction of things not seen."

Holman Christian Standard Bible-"Now faith is the reality of what is hoped for, the proof of what is not seen."

The Living Bible, Paraphrased—"What is faith? It is the confident assurance that something we want is going to happen. It is the certainty that what we hope for is waiting for us, even though we cannot see it up ahead."

The Amplified Bible—"Now faith is the assurance (the confirmation, the title-deed) of the things [we] hope for, being the proof of things [we] do not see and the conviction of their reality—faith perceiving as real fact what is not revealed to the senses."

Faith is complete confidence, wonderful assurance, seeing that which God has convinced us He wants us to accomplish as being accomplished. Faith is believing Him so much that we believe He is definitely going to do it. Anyone can believe a previously established fact. Faith is believing the advanced assurance God has given us as much as we believe established fact.

Faith is envisioning—and here Webster's dictionary fits faith exactly—"to have a mental image of, especially in advance of realization." How could you better describe faith? That's the quality God's great men have always possessed. They have looked to the future, seen God's goals, believed so much as to envision God accomplishing the task through them—and rejoiced both before and after God did it.

God's "greats" find a thrill in even thinking about faith. Trouble approaches, and it is but an opportunity for God to perform a miracle. A problem arises, and there is praise that God is doing such great things Satan had to attempt interference. A burden afflicts and prayer is offered, thanking God He is our great burden-bearer. Personal suffering approaches, only to find the believer saying, "Lord, I thank You that the sufferings of this world are not even worthy to be compared with the glory which shall be revealed hereafter" (Rom. 8:18).

Believe God for the Big Thing

Had someone said to Caesar, "Speak to the Roman Senate over a radio—a machine that can throw your voice across the airwaves," Caesar would have said, "Impossible."

Had someone said to Homer, "Why write with a pen? Why don't you type your Iliad on a computer?" After an explanation was given, Homer would have said, "Impossible."

Had someone said to Nero, "Ride from Naples to Rome in a machine that flies through the air," he would have said, "Impossible."

Had someone said to the Wright brothers, "A jet engine can carry your plane even faster," they would have thought, "Impossible."

History has now recorded that the very things thought impossible in centuries past are realities in our day. Things have a way of seeming impossible for a while, and then some time passes, and God's person of accomplishment comes along.

If an ordinary person desires to be used of God and will pay the price to be used, God can afford to work through him with tremendous power.

> *God often specializes in doing big things in history's very dark hours.*

We are too often content with little when God would give us much. Who said the great things of God have all been accomplished? In our hearts we should believe the best songs may yet be written; the best poems may yet be penned; the best sermons may yet be preached; the best lives may yet be lived; the best soul-winner may yet be found; the best person of faith may yet be uncovered. God often specializes in doing big things in history's very dark hours.

The Chase

God wants you: Believe God for the big thing! God has so many lives He could change because of your life: Believe God for the big thing! God has dreams and goals He knows could be accomplished for His glory through your life: Believe God for the big thing!

Life is too short to be content with mediocrity. It is not enough to be what others are, or to do something because everybody is doing it. In the extraordinary age in which you live, when some are dreaming extraordinary dreams, carry life's Textbook by your side, and life's Greatest Companion in your heart as your constant source of strength, and—be something besides ordinary. Believe God for the big thing.

Noah dared to believe God for the big thing, and built an ark. But what if Noah had not? *Abraham* dared to believe God for the big thing and left Ur, not knowing whither he went. But what if Abraham had not? *Joseph* dared to believe God for the big thing, and believed God would deliver him from plots as well as prisons. But what if Joseph had not? *Moses* dared to believe God for the big thing, and headed toward Egypt to rescue the Jews. But what if Moses had not?

David dared to believe God for the big thing, and marched boldly out to meet Goliath. But what if David had not? *Hezekiah* dared to believe God for the big thing, and on his knees prayed for an extension of lifespan. But what if Hezekiah had not? *Jeremiah* dared to believe God for the big thing, and went out to buy a field to prove it. But what if Jeremiah had not?

Daniel dared to believe God for the big thing, and opened his windows three times a day to pray toward Jerusalem. But what if Daniel had not? *Shadrach, Meshach, and Abednego* dared to believe God for the big thing, and asked Him for protection from a burning fiery furnace. But what if they had not? If these men had not believed God for the big thing, God would never have worked the big thing in their lives. Someone else might have stepped in willing to be used, but these would have been forgotten and buried in the sands of time.

> ***Believe God for the big thing!***

Attacks on Faith

Faith is positive; hence, negatives will attack and seek to destroy it.

C. S. Lovett tells of the time he and Dewey Lockman and Dr. Franklin Logsdon went to see Dr. Charles E. Fuller, preacher on the "Old Fashioned Revival Hour." In the course of the conversation, the name of a prominent Christian leader was mentioned, one who was then attacking Fuller Seminary. "I shall never forget Brother Fuller's response to the comment this man made about his school."

"Yeeesss," he drawled. "God bless him."

"Dr. Logsdon was the quickest to respond, 'You don't seem too upset, Brother Fuller!'"

"Then came an astonishing reply: 'Why should I let someone else decide how I am going to act!'"[1]

When faith gets attacked, it will often be attacked by temper, or hatred, or strife, and just enough to give you a good case of the "doubts." Just enough to block all your advances in the area of faith.

Watch for the negatives. A sign appeared on a city bus in downtown New York: "Doctors tell us that hating people can cause: ulcers, heart attacks, headaches, skin rashes, high blood pressure, and asthma." Someone had scrawled beneath it, "It doesn't make the people you hate feel good either."

Faith is the road to big things; hence, fear will seek to destroy it.

Fear makes faith flounder. Faith that flounders has lost its power and, of course, accomplishes nothing. Floundering faith will appear to be going somewhere and of course, goes nowhere. God cannot bless a life once fear has occupied God's throne chair. "God hath not given us the spirit of fear," Paul admonishes Timothy, "but of power, and of love, and of a sound mind" (2 Tim. 1:7 KJV).

Faith is the road to success; hence, defeated friends will seek to sidetrack you.

When God wishes to do something big, He often gives the dream to only one person. Years ago I heard a statement that quickly caught my attention, "If Satan cannot defeat you, he will defeat someone whose defeat will defeat you." I would barely modify it and say, "If the devil cannot defeat you, he will defeat someone whose defeat will attempt to defeat you." The attack on faith may come from well-meaning friends who simply have no desire to be used of God themselves, or even from family members. The one who walks by faith must expect to sometimes walk all alone.

Faith refuses to base itself on feelings; hence, feelings will attack from all sides.

Great Christians refuse to major on feelings. They major on faith. Any Christian always interested in his feelings will never amount to much for God. Until he gets his eyes off himself and onto Christ and a needy world, he will miss all the big goals God has for him. When Thomas said, "If I can see, I'll believe," he was not exercising faith, but doubt. When a Christian moves by feelings instead of by faith, he too has chosen to exercise doubt.

Faith refuses to acknowledge doubt; hence, doubt does everything possible to gain inroads through the questioning process.

Attacks on faith-goals do come. Always remember, if God gave you those goals after prayer, then faith will look far beyond all question marks and believe. Faith opens the door for His extraordinary power.

Dr. Adrian Rogers made a powerful statement that can speak to all of us when we find ourselves and our faith in limbo. *"Sometimes we die, not because of the hardening of the arteries, but because of the hardening of the attitude."*[2]

24

EXPERIMENT STATIONS AND RESEARCH CENTERS – DO THEY REALLY DONATE THEIR LIVES TO RESEARCH?

The Lord Jesus claims the use of your body, your whole being, your complete personality, so that as you give yourself to Him through the eternal Spirit, He may give Himself to you through the eternal Spirit, that all your activity as a human being on earth may be His activity in and through you; that every step you take, every word you speak, everything you do, everything you are, may be an expression of the Son of God, in you as man.[1]
—W. Ian Thomas

We must look out that our humility is not indolence with a solemn countenance upon it, the real fact being that we are content with the lowest place in heaven because we have not energy and self-sacrifice enough to make us strive after the highest.[2]
—A. J. Gordon

Our age is the age of science. In the days we have been alive, God has taught us a thousand things from His vast storehouse of knowledge. One of the sidelights of scientific advancement has been the discovery of the thrill involved in research and experimentation. Reflection will reveal:

For the sake of science, test pilots have tested the heavens—higher, higher, and still higher.

For the sake of science, astronomers have counted their lives as nothing, but have given themselves to scan the stars a thousand nights. For the sake of science, mathematicians have created advanced math, talked in new terminology, wrestled new formulas into being so man could scan the universe.

For the sake of science, many men and women have dedicated themselves to be hidden twelve hours a day in a research laboratory, simply to uncover secrets heretofore unknown.

For the sake of science, astronauts have been shot into space with the thrust of unbelievably powerful missiles right beneath their spaceship.

For the sake of science, male and female astronauts have become human experiments for heretofore untested lengths of time to see what seemingly impossible tasks could be accomplished while orbiting the world in the International Space Station.

For the sake of science, men have walked on the moon, and the volunteers wanting to go have always exceeded the number needed.

Risk—what about the risk of these experiments? Though it sounds scary to the rest of us, risk is viewed totally different by these people. Even if the amount of risk is astronomical, and the frequency of it unbelievable, still, risk is not an over-riding factor in their decision-making process. Apparently there is not much hesitation or lack of courage in those seeking to be personalized research centers or experiment stations—regardless of the cost. In fact, it would seem in many cases, the higher the risk involved, the higher the number of those seeking the job. There is something daringly wonderful about being in experimental work. The dedicated scientist seems to say, "Whether I live or die is not important, but the advancement of science is all that matters. If I can but add to the progress of mankind, my life will not have been in vain."

Why has science advanced so fast? Because of these personalized research centers.

Abundance of Surprises

When a child of God, filled with the Spirit, begins to allow God to stretch his dreams, and he ventures boldly into the arena of faith excitingly believing God, he is in for an abundance of surprises.

One surprise is the excitement of newly discovered power. No longer is he someone trying to do something for God. He is now someone who is trusting God to do something through him. Boundaries change. No longer is he limited to what he can accomplish in human strength. Now he will discover what God can accomplish with divine strength. He discovers it is "not me" but "Christ in me," not "my weakness" but "His strength," not "my problems" but "His opportunities," not "my needs" but "His inexhaustible storehouse of supply."

Another surprise is the excitement of new eyesight. He trades in the old eyes of human vision and begins to see things through God's eyes. "For we walk by faith, not by sight." Faith is a far better set of glasses than the believer has ever known before. Twenty-twenty vision can only satisfy until a believer knows there is something even better. What a blessing the day he tires of living by feeling and begins the new adventure of living by faith!

Another surprise is that the promises of God come fantastically alive. Promises heretofore hidden become treasure-chests, and each day unveils a new promise from God's thousands in His Word. The Bible is no longer just history. It is His-story. The promises become as up-to-date as the morning newspaper. A promise made in the first century becomes wonderfully applicable in the 21st century.

Could spiritual boredom ever change over to spiritual excitement? That's a tough question. Imagine a scenario like this…

Church had been a drudgery for Sam. He soon discovered it was not quite so bad if he missed one Sunday out of three. Sunday night was out of the question. A later revelation came to him, that if he would turn on the TV or go online, he could skip worshipping God with his wife and kids and other church attenders. In fact, he could even skip church for 3 Sundays out of 4, and still be able to tell his wife and fellow workers the next morning that he had heard a good sermon the day before. He didn't have to tell them he had read the comics, drank his coffee and shaved while the sermon was being streamed online. He could also boast to himself about how good he was at using his time and how great he was at multi-tasking.

Does God ever surprise anyone by changing spiritual boredom into spiritual excitement? That's probably another one of His specialties. Let's think about the human mind. Recently, on the television evening news, a reporter began sharing about an event that had just happened at a major American airport. The story was about a control tower employee who had gone to sleep on the job. Pilots called in for directions, anxious to know what to do. No answer! Planes had to land on their own—there was no answer from anyone in the tower to give advice on whether or when or where the pilot could land the plane. In the weeks that followed, there were more reports of one or two other controllers sleeping on the job. The reporter noted that some Air Traffic Controllers work long hours, sometimes alone! How important is an air-traffic controller? He may be the most important person in that part of the city. He has a major role in whether or not thousands of people stay alive! So a decision was quickly made. There must be two air-traffic-controllers in the tower at each major airport.

The human mind is a control center. Each of us has been given a God-given life, a God-given mind, and along with that, a God-given ability to influence our own actions and even affect the lives of others.

What a thought! Christ in the control tower of our life—not only as our Savior, but also as our Lord! In your mind, have you given Him that role? When Jesus is Lord, the believer then can see himself in a new light and every day carries the potential of new thrill. The believer is able to say: Jesus Christ lives in me through His Holy Spirit. He is eager to show me what He can accomplish through my life. My role is a new one now. I am His experiment station, His research center. Some of what He wants to accomplish in this world, He may wish to accomplish through me.

The Believer—A Research Center

I am His research center! Not that God needs to travel down new roads. He has already been down all of the roads before. But day by day He allows me to walk down new paths of usefulness to Him. "Hey, that's exciting. God, You mean You would use me!"

Of course He will use you . . . if you're usable! Why do you suppose He came to live in your life through the Holy Spirit? He has taken up residence inside of you. He is Lord of all life, wanting to use your life to the maximum.

Every believer should be God's personal research center and experiment station. When Paul shared with the Colossians that "Christ [is] in you, the hope of glory," he quickly became more specific saying, "Christ works in me mightily" (Col. 1:27, 29).

Abraham readily threw a knapsack on his back and headed out from his home to become an experiment station. Through his life God would show how many blessings can come to the man of faith.

Moses submitted to God to become an experiment station in the presence of Pharaoh himself. Through his life, for generations Egypt would remember the power of one man plus God.

Joshua didn't care who laughed when he shared his battle plan for conquering Jericho. He believed he was to be God's experiment station for conquering the Promised Land.

Rahab, sick of sin, turned to God and allowed Him to show the world how God could even change a harlot.

Ruth bravely put her neck on the line to pave the way for her Gentile world to follow the true God.

The Chase

Elijah experimented with challenging idolatry. He allowed God to use him to walk boldly into the enemy camp and challenge Baal worship in a Mount Carmel Super Bowl.

Daniel thrilled when God chose him to answer the question, "What's a man of God to do in a lion's den?"

The Hebrew children became personal research centers for the article, "How to Walk Through a Fiery Furnace."

Peter experimented with using a simple testimony and preaching to people from several other countries who gathered in Jerusalem for the Jewish feast day of Pentecost.

Paul became God's guinea pig for first-century missionary work. He asked Christ to use him to share the truth, hundreds of miles away from Tarsus. He was not even afraid to go to Rome.

Barnabas researched how to help discouraged young men like John Mark regain their composure and become giants for God.

Dwight Moody explored Sunday School work among needy kids of Chicago. An experiment in how to make Godly usage of adversity and prison cells was John Bunyan's project. David Livingstone became a research center to explore the villages of Africa where no white man had ever been. William Carey so had Christ in his heart he headed for India and became a pioneer in Bible translation of various languages and dialects. Bill Borden of Yale (1909) dreamed not of the million dollars he had in the bank but of sharing his excitement about the thrills Jesus Christ could bring into an individual life. He loved Muslims and was excited about getting to share Christ among Muslims on the other side of the world.

All of these simply discovered that one of the most exciting things in the world is to have God use you. There is no life more adventuresome than that of the believer who can say with Paul, "Christ is in me, and works in me mightily."

Rules for the Research Center

1. God utilizes no draftees. He calls, but all who are to have His power working through them are strictly volunteers.
2. Those used today are not certain of being used tomorrow. Before a vessel can be used, it must be "clean, fit for the Master's use."[3]
3. God shares His glory with no man. The one who is used of God and then takes credit and praise for doing what God did may well be overlooked in the days ahead.
4. God always provides His power when man is ready for it. The person who believes opportunities are "passing him by" needs to reassess whether he is totally yielded to God's control. The same one who believes "the harvest is plentiful, but the laborers are few"[4] is not about to overlook usable instruments. He has never overlooked even one.

Excitement That Endures

Occasionally someone may question whether it pays to serve Jesus. Students might ask, "What's in it for me? Suppose I do become God's research center and allow Him to accomplish His will in my life, what can I expect?"

Forrest Lowry started talking about some of his daily thrills. Not able to go and visit others, he laughed and said, "You know, I just tell the Lord to send the needy to my door and He does. I can't wait to see who is coming next!" He commented, "You know the Devil doesn't have any happy old people. I've never seen a one."

My mind reverted to years I spent on Seminary Hill in Fort Worth. The young people were excited, thrilled, having fun, serving as research centers, and preparing to go out to serve Jesus Christ around the world. However, the huge number of students around the campus were not always the ones with the greatest joy. One group on campus amazed many of us who were students.

They were the missionaries who had retired after many years of service in some distant country. They would drift back to Seminary Hill, and rent homes within walking distance. Most every day a few of them might show up at the chapel service, or visit in the classrooms, or relax in the Student Center. Some were the troops who had pioneered in the hard countries—the difficult areas—where the going had been unbelievably tough. Yet there they were, thrilled to be around the Seminary, thrilled to be alive, ready to share their stories if called on.

Put it all together. Serving as an experiment station for Jesus Christ allows one to come to the end of life with thrill and joy. Whether twenty-five or eighty-five, every day can be an exciting prayer: "Father, just think—a brand new day. I face this day with the awareness that Jesus Christ is alive in my life. Christ lives in me! Lord, what would You like to see accomplished in the town where I live today? I am Your research center. Walk through my feet, work through my hands, think through my brain, speak through my lips, and win through my sharing.

"I am Yours, Lord. Meet needs, lift burdens, bring joy, and save souls today as You work through me. I cannot do it, but You can. I am not able, but You are. I do not have the ability, but You do. And I thank You that You live in me, and desire to work in my life today."

Game Plan

Success is being what God wants you to be, and achieving what God wants you to achieve. It is only natural to expect there should be a "Game Plan" for achievement.

G **God's Fullness.** So as not to work in human power, so as not to be just what I can be in human strength, but so I can be all I can be in His strength, I must have God's fullness, the daily infilling of His Spirit, the daily cleansing He provides, the daily leadership He provides as He occupies the throne chair in my life.

A **Aims.** These are the goals. Once I only thought of my goals. No more. His goals are the only ones that can build a better world.

M **Motivation.** Christ is not just in me to be, but in me to do. When I have exhaled (thrust out the old, the sinful, the smudged page) and put it under His cross, I can believe the magnificent promise of 1 John 1:9. When I have spiritually inhaled, I have made the new surrender of the throne chair to Christ, gained anew the realization He knows how to direct my life much better than I do. Now from within He motivates, excites my spirit, counts my problems as His opportunities, shares in response to my asking His desires for the day, and I experience His power to accomplish all of it.

E **Envision.** By faith I can believe that what He challenges me to do, He is able to get done. Failure is not His motto. Self fails, but Christ succeeds. Now I can look at the challenge He assigned, and envision the goal being reached, the assignment carried out. Through the eyes of faith I can see it achieved.

There's the game plan. He's the coach. I'm excited about that. But there's more. He has allowed me to be on the team. In the most thrilling day of history, I'm on the team. In the day of the most challenges ever, I'm on the team. In the day when the opponent is displaying unusual toughness, I'm on the team. In that day the Coach has sent me in to play. In the day when it seems God has chosen to manifest His might more than ever before, I'm on the team.

The Chase

Perhaps once you said, "God chose me?" There need be no doubt about that. He put you here, didn't He? He matched you with this generation, didn't He? Turn your question mark to an exciting exclamation point, "God chose me!"

Don't you want in on what God is up to? He says, "You can do it. That's why I put you here. Have a go at it!"

Caution Lights in Usefulness

1. Don't miss the main assignment. We are not filled with God's power to neglect the main assignment. The main assignment given to believers is in Matthew 28:19–20 and Acts 1:8. Less than 24 hours prior to Calvary, Jesus stated one truth three different times:

"He who abides in Me, and I in him, he bears much fruit" (John 15:5). "By this is My Father glorified, that you bear much fruit, and so prove to be my disciples" (v. 8). "You did not choose me, but I chose you, and appointed you, that you should go and bear fruit, and that your fruit should remain"(v. 16). Sharing Christ with others should be of prime importance in the life of the believer.

2. No believer is stronger than his prayer life. Victories are won in the prayer closet. "Apart from me you can do nothing" (John 15:5) means that Satan will do everything possible to keep you from daily prayer appointments with God or to hinder your mind while praying.

3. Stay in the Word of God. "So faith comes from hearing, and hearing by the word of Christ" (Rom. 10:17). God simply does not seem to use Christians as research centers if they neglect His Word.

4. Major on faith, not feeling. Satan is a past master at moving emotions. Do not assume emotional jags mean God had chosen to use you. A wise man stated, "God expects spiritual fruit, not religious nuts." Rely on the promises of God and allow Him to use you to reach others for His glory.

5. God can accomplish much more through an army than through an individual. Occasionally, a Christian gets to feeling his importance and senses he doesn't need the local church. You may not need your church, but you need some church. Find a church where the Bible is preached, and believed, and where Christians radiate Christ in everyday excitement. But by all means have a church! Of the more than 100 times the word "church" is used in the New Testament, more than 90 of these usages refer to a specific local church in a specific local setting. Christians are involved in a war with the devil, and the devil would love to try to get a Christian to be a one-man army!

6. Expect God to use you if you are Spirit-filled. It is an astounding fact that some people sell out to Christ and then seem surprised that God would use them. Expect Him to use the available, usable tool. God never runs out of job assignments.

When you are not being used, don't doubt God. Remember the conversation (chapter 20) between the two missionaries. God often does special things when the believer stays totally yielded and totally usable.

25

THE KEY TO PERMANENT MOTIVATION

You can find fault with Moses, and with Abram, and with Job, and with Isaiah, and with David, and with Paul, and with Barnabas. You can put your finger on the defects of men up and down the world, without any exception; but Christ alone stands flawless, spotless, and without sin. You cannot say that about any other life. His life attests His divine claims.

—George W. Truett

Wherever the true message of Jesus Christ has gone, people have been revolutionized, resulting in new life, new hope, and new purpose for living. Indeed, without fear of contradiction, we can regard Jesus Christ as history's greatest revolutionary. Everything about Him was unique: The prophecies of His coming, His birth, His life, His teachings, His miracles, His death, His resurrection, His influence on history and in the lives of hundreds of millions of people.

—Dr. Bill Bright [1]

Is there a way to be continually motivated? Is it feasible to be a long-term achiever? Is it possible to experience motivation that lasts? Think about Jesus—the great motivator!

Dr. Bill Bright wrote a book with this title and subtitle:

A Man Without Equal
JESUS, THE MAN WHO CHANGED THE WORLD

199

Ever wondered about this? God loved you so much that He sent His Son, the greatest motivator who ever walked the earth, to tell you how to be saved and how to be motivated all through this life, and then forever.

Thirty-three short years on earth! In that span of time, Jesus continually reached that achievement of being the person God wanted Him to be. Not once did He fail. In addition, He continually achieved the goals that the Father wanted Him to accomplish in those years. Frequently Jesus was tempted to turn aside and formulate some selfish goals. He steadfastly refused. Only the goals God wanted accomplished in His life were the ones He pursued, the ones He chased. While He lived, men listened to His magnificent teaching and exclaimed, "Never man so spoke."[2] Ever since His death, men have been studying His life only to conclude, "Never man so lived."

Napoleon said, "I know men; and I tell you that Jesus Christ is no mere man. Between Him and every other person in the world there is no possible term of comparison. Alexander, Caesar, Charlemagne, and I have founded empires. But on what did we rest the creations of our genius? Upon force. Jesus Christ founded His empire upon love; and at this hour millions of men would die for Him."[3]

Herbert Lockyer remarks: "He never wrote a book, and yet all the libraries of the country could not hold the books that have been written about Him. He never wrote a song, and yet He has furnished the theme for more songs than all the song writers combined. He never founded a college, but all the schools put together cannot boast of having as many students."[4]

An unknown author wrote, many years ago, "Centuries have come and gone, and today Jesus is the centerpiece of the human race, and the leader of all human progress. I am well within the mark when I say that all the armies that ever marched, all the navies that were ever built, all the parliaments that have ever sat, and all the kings that have ever ruled put together have not affected the life of man upon this earth like this one solitary personality."

Motivation Expert

Bruce Barton shares his opinion of the motivating ability of Jesus in The Man and the Book Nobody Knows.

> He did not overthrow the oppressive government of Rome. He did not lower the tax rate. He did not improve sanitary conditions in Jerusalem, nor did He erect a public library in Nazareth. He did not increase the wages of Christians over those of infidels. He taught no sure cure for disease. The economic status of His followers was exactly as it had been: He found them fishermen, He left them fishermen. . . .
>
> But His fishermen were different men, transformed, endowed with power, capable of great faith and magnificent achievement. Through them and their successors He started more philanthropies than all others who have ever lived. Hospitals and clinics, charities and libraries, schools and colleges have multiplied where He has inspired the souls of men. His religion is the best asset of civilization. That part of the world outside of which very few of us would willingly spend our days is named for Him, Christendom.[5]

Without a doubt, the master motivator of all time has been Jesus of Nazareth. Others have spoken of doing it, but Jesus did it and continues to do it. He has instilled more confidence, brought more joy, thrilled more lives, excited more hearts, and moved more men to action than any other man who has ever lived.

Motivation is never automatic. The individual who is not motivated cannot motivate. The one who is not moved to action himself is not going to move anyone else to action, at least not for long. The question worth asking is, "Who motivated the earthly Jesus?" What was there about Jesus that set Him aside from the crowd?

It was obvious that He was…
Confident
A dreamer
An extraordinary goal achiever
Filled with the power of God
Loaded with love
Yet bold and brave.

Special Qualities of a Special Life

The most successful person who ever lived was also the most spiritual person. From the outset of His public ministry, the Bible indicates Jesus was filled with the Holy Spirit. Luke records, "And Jesus, full of the Holy Spirit, returned from the Jordan, and was led about by the Spirit in the wilderness."[6]

After the temptations the secret is again shared—"And Jesus returned to Galilee in the power of the Spirit." When He came to Nazareth after He began His public ministry, He went into the synagogue, and the passage He chose to read began, "The Spirit of the Lord is upon me."[7]

Years later, with Jesus long since gone, the writer of Acts mentions "You know of Jesus of Nazareth, how God anointed Him with the Holy Spirit and with power, and how He went about doing good, and healing all who were oppressed by the devil, for God was with Him."[8]

We need to learn all we can from the life of Jesus. We chase after something called success, and hopefully, we have a desire to reach all the goals God has for us.

Why not chase the qualities that were in the life of Jesus?

S	Spirit-filled
U	Usable
C	Courageous
C	Confident
E	Enthusiastic
S	Submitted
S	Sharing with others

SPIRIT-FILLED. Jesus stayed alone in prayer until the power of God literally absorbed every portion of His life. He was never anxious to just attract the multitudes. He was anxious to be totally absorbed with the power of God. If needs be, He would leave thousands to push apart, go across the lake and find a place to pray.

USABLE. Jesus determined to be a vessel, clean, fit for the Father's use. He was "one who has been tempted in all things as we are, yet without sin" (Heb. 4:15). Is it any wonder God could use Him? The unusual thing would have been for God not to use Him. The natural thing for God is always to use the usable vessel.

COURAGEOUS. Money changers with exorbitant interest rates had best stay out of the Temple area when Jesus came to town, for He always possessed an abundance of courage. When He felt something was God's will, He would move into the arena of battle to accomplish it.

CONFIDENT. Jesus never lacked confidence. He believed He could, by the power of God, accomplish exactly what God wanted Him to accomplish. Not once did Jesus move about with indecisiveness. Because He knew His heart was right and His goals were right, He moved about with unswerving confidence. His confidence was not false confidence, it came from the fact that He was competent to do all He had been designed to do.

ENTHUSIASTIC. The root of "enthusiasm" is the Greek word enthousiasmos. This word comes from two smaller Greek words, en theos, meaning "in God." The greatest kind of enthusiasm comes when one knows he is "in God." There is deep inner excitement and thrill. Jesus possessed a fantastic enthusiasm not only to live the abundant life, but to share it.

SUBMITTED. One reason God could afford to fill Jesus with power was because Jesus was totally submitted to the will of God. The person who is not submissive will be put on the shelf. God has a way of simply moving on by that person to use another. A study of the prayer Jesus prayed in Gethsemane is an excellent example of total submission.

SHARING WITH OTHERS. Watch Jesus at work. He was always helping people, always seeking to lift the depressed out of their defeat, always seeking to lead individuals to a right relationship with God. Great goals! On two different occasions, the Father spoke from Heaven saying, "This is my beloved Son, with whom I am well-pleased."[9]

It is time we learned that when one can enjoy life, as Jesus did; help people on every hand, as Jesus did; lift hundreds out of defeat, lead many to a right relationship with God, as Jesus did; and hear God say He is well-pleased, as Jesus did; then that person has discovered the true meaning of success.

Jesus was successful. To Jesus, success was being the person God intended for Him to be, and achieving the goals God intended that He achieve. Everything Jesus did was oriented in this one basic context. Having set His goals in the place of prayer, He would refuse to be satisfied until each one was accomplished. A Bible concordance will reveal that the word "must" was an often used word in His vocabulary. At age twelve the impelling inner drive was "I must be about my Father's business." When one says "must," as Jesus frequently did, it is an indication that goals are set, eyes will not be turned aside, and the person is goal-oriented toward successful achievement. Jesus was aiming for spiritual success.

Fulfilling the Main Purpose

As great as it was for Jesus to know that the Father was well-pleased with His life on earth, Jesus knew the main purpose for which He had come to earth. Before He had been born into this life, the angel of the Lord had appeared to Mary and stated that purpose. He would save people from their sins.[10] Shepherds also would receive a special message, telling "good news of great joy which shall be for all the people. A Savior had been born that day, who was Christ the Lord."[11] Immediately after a tax-collector named Zaccheus gave great evidence of having just been saved, Jesus stated His long-range goal to Zaccheus—"for the Son of Man has come to seek and save the lost."[12]

Now the time had come. To do the will of God for Jesus meant He was to fulfill the plan that God had started after Adam and Eve experienced sin in the Garden of Eden. In the last week of His earthly life, Jesus prayed a long prayer. "Father, the hour has come; glorify Thy Son, that the Son may glorify Thee."[13] He knew that the cross was just ahead, that the great plan for seeing people saved had been started in Heaven, and He knew that He, Jesus, was to be the fulfillment of it. He had announced that plan earlier—that the Father God loved the people of the world so much, that He sent His Son Messiah Jesus, so that whoever would truly repent and believe in Him would be saved, and saved forever (everlasting life).[14]

Paul said—"God demonstrated His own love toward us, in that while we were still sinners, Christ died for us."[15] John, another of the disciples, was very close to Jesus, and decades later John would write that Christ's payment was for our sins, but not for ours only, but also for those sins of the whole world."[16] To achieve what God wanted Him to achieve, Jesus would die. He died in a cruel death on a wooden cross.

That's not the end of the story. God raised Him up again, raised Jesus from the dead. The excitement-level in His followers would explode. They could tell the story of Jesus.

When Times Got Tough--One Big Dreamer Failed

Jesus—the great Motivator! Jesus—the Father's solution for the sins of every person on earth! Could anyone who had big dreams about following Jesus just suddenly fail? Yes, Simon Peter could and did fail. He was one of the key disciples. He failed the same way many big achievers and many would-be-big-achievers fail. Colossal failure can suddenly appear. The question is "Why?" Why did Simon Peter fail? Self-centered ego! Seeking to protect himself—He denied being a follower of Jesus, even saying plainly, "I do not know Him."[17]

Peter knew how to be bold—earlier. He seemed to be a self-appointed spokesman, for Jesus. When Jesus asked a question, Peter knew—"You are the Messiah, the Son of the living God!"[18] Peter was excited about the name of Jesus—when he was with believers. Among unbelievers, when Jesus had been seized, on this one occasion, Peter caved in. The disciple John, I suspect, may have been Peter's best friend. Writing about Peter, many years later, John used these words about that sad night, and John used the same sad words twice, "Peter warmed himself."[19]

The eyes of Peter and the eyes of Jesus met that night. "The Lord turned and looked at Peter."[20] That look was all that was needed. Peter went out and wept bitterly.

Failure Does Not Have To Be Final

Repentance—real repentance? What is real repentance? To repent means to turn around, to go in the opposite direction. Real repentance is known, not only by what we say to God when we tell Him we are repenting, but also by how we act from that time forward. God knows when repentance is real, and God knows when repentance is not real.

Watch Simon Peter closely. No egocentric self-protection denials now. Or self-protecting silence. Within two months, Peter would be preaching, and when he was not publicly preaching, he was talking privately—about Jesus. He was always talking about Jesus, and telling people to repent.[21] As a result of one sermon Peter preached, 3,000 were saved at one time. Soon there were 5,000 believers, just among the men.

Peter and his friend John kept speaking about Jesus, and they both were amazed and excited. Jesus was alive! God had raised Him up!!! Peter kept repeating that phrase—over and over and over again![22]

And Peter shared the good results that came when there was true repentance—"repent...that your sins may be wiped out so that seasons of refreshing may come from the presence of the Lord..."[23]

Peter spent the rest of his life emphasizing the name of Jesus, and the importance of that name. "There is salvation in no one else; for there is no other name under heaven given to people by which we must be saved."[24]

Later he would write two letters. He starts his first letter by calling himself, "Peter, a bond servant and apostle of Jesus Christ." Toward the end of his last letter, Peter would share an exciting truth for people of every race and every nation. He wanted everyone to know—"The Lord is not wishing for any to perish, but for all to come to repentance."[25] Jesus had forgiven Peter, and He gave Peter the joy of further ministry— to bounce back and excitedly share more truth about the name of Jesus.

That one dreadful experience that Peter had was an experience that changed his life forever. The one thing we forget is that his tragic blunder became one of the several greatest learning experiences in his life. The lesson — Jesus had not only been a good motivator. Jesus is the key to permanent motivation! The best motivation may be totally overlooked if you miss the key to permanent motivation!

26

DREAM WITH GOD

You remember the time. If you are a true believer in Jesus Christ, you remember. What a thrill to recall how God was chasing you, drawing you with His conviction of sin, and His offer of salvation that would come with repentance and faith. Now there's more! You can have His power in your life, be used of Him and have and achieve the goals He has in mind for you. Look to discover where He is looking. Ask Him to use you in ways He desires. Dream with God!

—whc

"...let us run with endurance the race that is set before us, fixing our eyes on Jesus, the author and perfecter of faith." [1]

Have you ever considered that you could dream—with God? You are here because of the goodness of God. And God has a special plan for your life. Each of us needs to look for ways to discover those dreams or goals He has for us, and then fit ourselves into the unique plans He has in mind.

At times the heart cries out, "If only God would speak out loud!" And with excitement, we learn, He has! The Bible, the believer's handbook, can come alive and seem fresh each day for those who daily dig in. "The word of God is living and active, and sharper than any two edged sword...." [2]

The Bible shares several chapters of conversation that took place during the last week of the earthly life of Jesus. The disciples were gradually becoming more discouraged. What Jesus taught in His last tough week on earth was actually some great news for anyone facing discouragement, then or now. He spoke one truth after another—

"You did not choose Me, but I chose you, that you should go and bear fruit...[3]

"If I go away, I will send Him (the Holy Spirit) to you.[4]

"I will ask the Father, and He will give you another Helper, that He may be with you forever, the Spirit of truth . . . "[5]

". . . you know Him, because He abides with you, and will be in you."[6]

"I will not leave you as orphans, I will come to you."[7]

"In that day, you shall know that I am in my Father, and you in me, and I in you,"[8]

"In the world you shall have tribulation, but be of good cheer; I have overcome the world."[9]

"These things I have spoken to you, that in Me, you may have peace."[10]

Even though Jesus was about to endure the cross, He was thinking of you! He spoke not just of those who were following Him then, but of everyone that would come after them. Even when facing death, He was looking further into the future. We are told to be like Him, to "look unto Jesus...who for the joy that was set before Him endured the cross, despising the shame, and has sat down at the right hand of the throne of God."[11]

There Are New Discoveries to Make

It is never too soon to turn back to God–for a new dream or dreams, for a fresh vision, for a new plan to carry out any God-given vision, for seeking from Him new skills and new determination to put that plan into action or for praying new prayers for others!

It is never too soon to listen to what God is saying and put it into practice. Think of that word "success." That word came from God. God brought up the subject to Joshua. God had found in Joshua a younger man who was willing to be used, probably scared, but willing. And God said, *"Be strong and courageous... meditate on it (God's law) day and night, so that you may be careful to do according to do all that is written in it."* Success would center around both being and doing. And then God shares a great thought—*"then you will make your way prosperous, and then you will have success."*[12] God was strongly emphasizing, "Joshua, don't you miss the part that you play in the big jobs just ahead. And Joshua was listening very carefully.

It is never too soon to learn where the best dreams originate. Answer this huge question! Joshua's dream—where did that dream begin? Not with Joshua. Joshua's dream of what could be done through Joshua—started with God. God had the plan. Joshua was to be and to do his part of carrying out that plan, but Joshua was to remember all his life, that the plan began with God. God's dream and plan for Joshua was fixed, *before* it entered Joshua's mind and became Joshua's dream and plan. God has special plans for each of His servants, and each one is to seek to hear from God for himself.

Great Questions from a Great God

"The Bible is up-to-date and pertinent for today. Think about that. I think that means that when you read it, God seems to have something in the passage where you are reading that applies right then. You've probably had that experience, more than once. God hits you with it, and He applies it to your circumstance, right then, right at that special time.

Think of the first question God ever asked anyone.

"Where are you?"

If God made the universe and all things in it, didn't He know where Adam was? Yes, He knew! But Adam had sinned, disobeyed God, and gone into hiding. Even then, God's interest was still there. And Adam was going to learn the hard lesson—you can't hide from God. Adam had missed the mark. No better definition has ever been given for sin— sin is to miss the mark, to disobey God. One facet of this is to miss the purpose, miss the plan, for which you have been placed on this earth.

Adam knew he had missed it, and he admits he was hiding. He told God, "I hid myself."[13]

Notice how up-to-date the next question is.

"What are you doing here?"

God asked that of Elijah, not long after God had used the prophet in a great spiritual battle with false prophets and false gods on Mt. Carmel. Why, God? Why ask Elijah that? Didn't Elijah deserve a time-out, some days off? And wasn't he at Mt. Sinai, a good place for a spiritual retreat? God actually asked the question twice.[14]

Elijah was bone-weary, worn-out, tired, and wanted to retire. God was not finished with him. God's questions are reminders that He is always interested in us, old or young, in where we are and what we're doing.

To Elijah, it was like God saying, *"Elijah, I'm your Sovereign God. It's not time yet for you to ride in a chariot and be swept up to Heaven. Leave your retreat spot. I have more goals in mind for you. Get back with people. Rest comes later—when I take you home. Hang in there! I'm not through with you!"*

God wanted Elijah to invest some time in the life of Elisha, and some other younger prophets.[15] God invests in us, and we invest in others.

The Far-Reaching Vision of God

The interest of God had never been for just one nation. He wanted to be the Lord of all the nations, and wanted all those nations to have His great salvation.

The wide expanse of the vision of God is frequently shared in Scripture. To Abram, God said, "I will make you a great nation, and bless you . . . And in you *all the families of the earth shall be blessed.*"[16] In Psalm 67 they sang, "God, bless us...*that Thy way may be known on the earth, Thy salvation among all nations... Let the nations be glad and sing for joy.*"[17]

In the Old Testament, Joseph became powerful and influential in the land of Egypt. Jonah would be sent to preach about God's salvation in Nineveh. Daniel and Ezekiel became leaders in Babylon.

When the birth of Jesus was announced, it was *"good news of great joy...for all the people!"*[18] A multitude of angels praised God when Jesus was born and stated plainly, *"Glory to God in the highest, and on earth peace among men with whom He is pleased."* Wise men came from a far Eastern country saying, *"We have seen His star in the east, and have come to worship Him."*[19]

Jesus went to unpopular people groups, and many of those believed that He was the Messiah.[20]   One verse Jesus shared has come to be known and loved around the globe. *For God so loved the world that He gave His only begotten Son, that whoever believes in Him should not perish, but have eternal life."*[21]

God led Phillip to share the good news about Jesus with a man from Ethiopia. He led Paul to many different countries to preach the gospel of salvation. John wrote that *"we have an advocate who pleads our case before the Father. He is Jesus Christ, the One who is truly righteous. He Himself is the sacrifice that atones for our sins--and not only our sins but the sins of all the world.*"[22] Peter preached that the Lord is *"not wanting any to perish, but* **all** *to come to repentance."*[23] Many have quoted, *"Be still and know that I am God"* but the rest of the verse expands the meaning, *"I will be exalted among the* **nations**. *I will be exalted in* **the earth."**[24] Jesus gave a command to His followers—*"Go therefore and make disciples of all the nations."*[25]

What is God looking for? He is looking to have the leader's role in our personal goal-setting. In our day, He is looking for men, women, business people, political personalities, lawyers, doctors, professors, teachers, actors, homemakers, young couples, singles, university students, high schoolers, middle schoolers, younger boys and girls—individuals willing and wanting to be used. He is seeking those who will not just *call* Jesus Lord—but they will let Him *be* Lord in their lives each day. Wherever you go, in your business, in your daily walk, in your life, remember—God wants to reach all people groups with the message of Jesus Christ. And He wants to use you!

Ordinary Individuals—They Dreamed with God

Think of some of those people in the Bible—the ones God used! Think of some that He used in extraordinary ways. Nearly all of them lived in very difficult days. They saw evil deeds going on around them and must have wondered what was going to happen next. Did they ever experience anxiety about their future? Did they ever get scared?

We know that God worked, that He wonderfully and powerfully worked to achieve His goals through some of those individuals. Why did God use them? They chased His goals. They were willing to put their lives on the line and dream big dreams with God. I wonder if any of them ever prayed common prayers, like these . . .

Abram—"God, I've never even been very far away from my town,

Ur. But You said 'Go.' God, You haven't told me my final destination. Help me with my faith. Will You lead me?"

Moses—"I'm sure not a leader, nor am I a good speaker. But I heard You loud and clear when that bush was on fire, yet it didn't burn up. I'm scared, but let's go."

Noah—"I don't have great skills when it comes to construction work. And I've never heard of any building project like this boat You're thinking of. I've never even seen it rain. But . . . if You think I can do it, I'm willing to try."

Joshua—"Are You sure I'm Your man? I'm certainly not Moses. Did You just say something about having good success? Who, me?"

Rahab—"I have literally ruined my life. No one could fall lower than I have. And no one has ever come to my door to help me up. Until now. But I do know this one thing, God. I want to be on Your side. You're real."

Hannah—"I've been crying so hard. I can't even eat. I just want a child. I'd give anything to have one. I promise You—I'll dedicate him to You—for life."

Elisha—"God, Elijah's been a good mentor. But I'm not like him. I would need a double portion of Your spirit and power if I'm to be used at all."

Ruth—"I'm going to stick with my mother-in-law. She needs me. We have no money. But like I told Naomi, 'I want her God to be my God.'"

Shadrach, Meshach, Abednego—"We're three scared young guys, God. First, they stole us from our country. Now they are going to put us in a hot furnace to kill us. But we're Yours, God. We will not bow to any image."

Young Daniel—"I know the new law says I can't pray except to the king, but I'm just going to keep kneeling at my open window three times a day. I know I may be thrown in with the lions, but God, I have to keep praying to You—and only You."

The Chase

Simon Peter—"I'm the guy known for having a big mouth. I confess that I've been arrogant, and I've said the wrong things. Today's a feast day called Pentecost. There are lots of people around. What if this time I asked You to use my big mouth? Would You help me tell them about Jesus, about His death, and His resurrection?" God, would You help me use my big mouth in the right way, today?

Luke—"It's good to be a doctor and help people. And I really thank You, God, for the opportunities You give me to talk about Jesus—in the different countries controlled by Rome."

Paul—"That strong light made me blind. I'm still trembling. Who are You, Lord? You say You are Jesus? If You'll give me another chance to do Your will, I'll do it."

Jailer in Philippi—"God, that earthquake was for real. Thanks for saving my life. Now our whole family is going to follow You. And we will all get baptized too."

John Mark—"Lord, I failed on that first mission trip. God, are You truly the God of second chances? Would You give me one more chance?"

Epaphroditus—"I'm just a delivery guy, taking stuff to Paul. But God, is there any way You might use me while I'm over at Philippi."

Lois—"Lord, is there anything grandmothers can do? My daughter Eunice and I are working to teach her son, Timothy, the Scriptures."

Timothy—"I know I'm very young. But if You will just let me stay around Paul, and let him mentor me, I could learn a lot. I want to serve You, Lord."

John—"It's lonely out here on this Patmos island where they put me. Is there any way You could use me in this isolated place?"

Samuel as a child—"God, I thought that was Eli calling my name. But he said it must be You. I'm just going to say what he told me to say to You if I heard You again. So I'm saying it out loud, 'Speak, Lord, I'm listening.'"

David, as a teenager—"Lord, I know sheep. I know music. I play instruments, and I can write songs. I can also do some other amazing things with the hands and fingers you gave me. I sure want my songs and my fingers to please you. I'm just a shepherd, Lord, not even 20 years old yet. Do You have anything else that You want to do with me?"

Narrowing the Chase

Glance over that long list of names again. The ages of those in that list should begin to bring exciting new thoughts. God's dream for those of us here on earth does not seem to be limited by how old or young we are. Rather than calling His followers at one certain age, He was interested in each person—Samuel as a small boy, David as a teenager, Daniel as a very young man, Ruth as a young widow, and Lois as a grandmother. Moses was 80 when God called him and assigned him bigger goals than ever.

God began something important by planting a dream in their minds. They were ordinary people, like me, like you. God created human minds with His idea of stretching them.

Do not deify fear. Don't make a god out of fear—or hesitation. Hesitation, according to the dictionary, can mean to hold back in doubt or indecision. And hesitation can frequently bring more fear. Hesitation can get in the way and become a controlling substitute for some goal or dream God has been trying to get you to tackle. Brain freeze can become a reality.

Think again of those ordinary people in the list. Each one of those people had a reason to be afraid. But they would not give over to fear. They pursued and chased some goals they did not reach, like me, like you. But they each had a special moment when they listened and responded to the Lord—for life. So God was able to dream His dream, through them. Why? They dreamed with God.

Ask God to give you a dream of some goals He has for you— starting now. And no matter where you are in life—God has goals for you and is ready to stretch you. Paul was in his sixties, in a prison cell, being persecuted for his faith, and had plenty of think-time. He knew it was time to think about what else was to be involved in his chase. He had no desire to chase unimportant things. And he had never heard of retirement from continual goal-seeking or goal-reaching. So he talked of "…one thing I do." Forgetting what was in the past, he would reach forward to what God had for him out ahead. [26] He was narrowing his chase, narrowing the focus of his goals. Even in prison, still having an "I can do…" spirit [27], he wanted to be successful to the end, to continually succeed at any goals God would help him set.

You must begin with God. When you want to find your purpose, when you have a good question, when you are wondering about the future, when you are looking for ways to succeed—begin with God! "When you think about your schooling, when you think about your job, when you plan, when you look for a Godly marriage partner, when you try to establish a foundation for your family, when you are dealing with your children and their needs, begin with God! And when you are seeking to know the results can be tremendous for those who have followed God's plan and received Jesus Christ as Savior and Lord. Ravi Zacharias says that "Jesus offers the one who comes to Him—a chance to be what in ourselves we cannot be, and to do what by ourselves we cannot do."[28]

God's search is on. He is looking for ordinary individuals who want to be successful. "For the eyes of the Lord run to and fro throughout the whole earth, to show Himself strong on behalf of those whose heart is loyal to Him."[29] There are things He is ready to empower you to do. Ask God to dream some of His dreams through you!

Sources

(All Quotations from the Bible are from the NASB (New American Standard Bible) unless otherwise noted)

Chapter 1

1. Sharon Begley, Newsweek Magazine, "Brain Freeze, How the Deluge of Information Paralyzes
   Our Ability to Make Good Decisions," March 7, 2011.
2. Mrs. Edmund Craster
3. Luke 11:17
4. Proverbs 15:13, HCSB
5. Proverbs 15:30, NLTSE
6. Proverbs 15:15, HCSB

Chapter 2

1. Joshua 1:8
2. William H. Burnham, The Normal Mind, Reprinted by permission of Hawthorn Books, Inc., Copyright @ 1929 by D. Appleton & Co. All rights reserved.

Chapter 3

1. Maxwell Maltz, M.D., PsychoCybernetics (Englewood Cliffs, NJ: Prentice Hall, Inc., 1960), p. vi. Used by permission.
2. Genesis 1:4
3. Genesis 1:10
4. Genesis 1:12
5. Genesis 1:18
6. Genesis 1:25
7. Reprinted by permission from a tract, Good news Publishers, Westchester, IL: 60153.

8. Psalm 139:14

9. W. T. Conner, Revelation and God: An Introduction to Christian Doctrine (Nashville, TN: Broadman Press, 1936, Renewal, 1964), p. 51. Used by permission.

10. Ibid., pp. 5152.

11. A. H. Strong, Systematic Theology (Philadelphia: Judson Press, 1907), p. 514.

Chapter 5

1. Luke 12:13–21

2. Exodus 20:9

3. 1 Thessalonians 4:11-12, NLT

4. 2 Thessalonians 3:10-12, NLT

5. B. H. Carroll, Pastoral Epistles of Paul, I and 2 Peter, Jude, 1, 2, and 3 John, Vol. XVI: An Interpretation of the English Bible (Old Tappan, NJ: Fleming H. Revell Co., 1942), p. 331.

6. Ibid., pp. 33132.

7. Habakkuk 2:9-10

8. James 4:14

9. Ron Blue, Storm Shelter, (Nashville: Thomas Nelson Publishers, 1994), pp. 146-147.

Chapter 7

1. Mark 8:36

2. John 16:33

3. Galatians 6:3

4. Philippians 4:13

5. Luke 6:26

6. Keith Miller, A Second Touch. (Waco, Texas: Word Books,1968, pp. 54-55.

Chapter 8

1. Matthew 14:27

Chapter 9
1. John 14:27 (KJV)
2. 1 Peter 5:7
3. Andrew Murray, The New Life (Minneapolis: Bethany Fellowship, Inc., 1967), p. 105. Used by permission.
4. Ibid., p. 106.

Chapter 10
1. F. W. Farrar, The Life and Work of St. Paul (London: Cassell, Petter, Galpin, and Co., n.d.), II, p. 579.

Chapter 11
1. From "Working Well," July 1995, p. 4.

Chapter 12
1. Genesis 3:10
2. Maxwell Maltz, PsychoCybernetics, p. 25.
3. Luke 22:31-34 (paraphrase)
4. Robert Thouless, An Introduction to the Psychology of Religion (New York: Cambridge University Press, 1923), p. 52.
5. James Jauncey, This Faith We Live By (Grand Rapids: Zondervan Publishing Co., 1966), pp. 1415. Used by permission.
6. Robert Thouless, An Introduction to the Psychology of Religion (New York: Cambridge University Press, 1923), p. 53.
7. Oswald Chambers, My Utmost for His Highest (New York: Dodd, Mead, and Co., 1963), p. 250.
8. James 4:7
9. Ephesians 6:11
10. Isaiah 40:30-31
11. 1 John 4:4

The Chase

Chapter 13
1. John 6:35; 6:51; 7:38.
2. Mark 3:35
3. John 14:1

Chapter 14
1. John 14:12 (paraphrase)
2. Harold Wildish, The Glorious Secret, (Westchester, Illinois: Good News Publishers, 1963), p. 6.

Chapter 15
1. Bill Bright, "How To Be Filled with the Holy Spirit," New Life Publications, PO Box 593684, Orlando, FL 32859

Chapter 18
1. F. Marshall Brown, F. K. Berrien, David L. Russell, Applied Psychology (New York: The Macmillan Co., 1966), p. 380.

Chapter 19
1. 2 Corinthians 7:4
2. Joni Eareckson Tada, Seeking God, My Journey of Prayer and Praise. (Brentwood, TN: Wolgemuth and Hyatt, 1991).
3. Donald Grey Barnhouse, Let Me Illustrate (Westwood, New Jersey: Fleming H. Revell Co., 1967), p. 21.
4. 1John 1:3-4; 3John 4
5. Ron Blue, Storm Shelter (Nashville: Penguin Books), pp. 31-32.
6. Airline Passenger Association News (Summer/Fall 1972), pp. 2630.

Chapter 20
1. Dave Ramsey, The Money Answer, (Nashville, TN: Countryman Books),p. 116 shares this quotation

from Billy Graham

2. James McConkey, The Surrendered Life (Pittsburgh, Pennsylvania: Silver Publishing Co.).

Chapter 21

1. Dave Ramsey, More Than Enough, (New York: Penguin Books), p. 65.

2. Clyde Narramore, This Way to Happiness (Grand Rapids: Zondervan Publishing Co., 1958), p. 156. Used by permission.

3. Howard G. Hendricks, Elijah (Chicago: Moody Press, Moody Bible Institute, 1972), p. 19. Used by permission.

4. T.B. Maston, Right or Wrong, (Nashville: Broadman Press, 1955), pp. 29–46

Chapter 22

1. Ephesians 3:20, KJV

2. Acts 1:8, NASB

3. Donald Grey Barnhouse, Let Me Illustrate (Westwood, New Jersey: Fleming H. Revell Co., 1967), pp. 132-133.

Chapter 23

1. C. S. Lovett, Unequally Yoked Wives (Baldwin Park, Calif.: Personal Christianity Publishers, 1968), pp. 71–72.

2. Dr. Adrian Rogers, "Love Worth Finding" radio program message

Chapter 24

1. W. Ian Thomas, The Sating Life of Christ (Grand Rapids: Zondervan Publishing Co., 1962), p. 151. Used by permission.

2. A. J. Gordon, Great Pulpit Masters Series, Vol. VIII (New York: Fleming H. Revell Co., 1951), p. 66.

3. 2 Timothy 2:21

4. Matthew 9:37

The Chase

Chapter 25
1. Bill Bright, A Man Without Equal (Orlando, FL: New Life Publications, 1995), p. 15.
2. John 7:46
3. Frank S. Mead (ed.), Encyclopedia of Religious Quotations (New York: Revell Co., 1965), p. 56.
4. Herbert Lockyer, The Man Who Changed the World, Vol. I (Grand Rapids: Zondervan Publishing Co., 1967), p. 24. Used by permission.
5. 4 Bruce Barton, The Man and the Book Nobody Knows (New York: The Bobbs-Merrill Co., 1924, 1925, 1929, 1956, 1959), p. 214. Used by permission.
6. Luke 4:1
7. Luke 4:14, 18
8. Acts 10:38
9. Matthew 17:5
10. Matthew 1:19-25
11. Luke 2:10, HCSB
12. Luke 19:5-10
13. John 17:1
14. John 3:16
15. Romans 5:8, HCSB
16. 1 John 2:2
17. Luke 22:57
18. Matthew 16:16, HCSB
19. John 18:18,25
20. Matthew 16:75; Luke 22:62
21. Acts 2:38; 3:19; 8:20-25; 2 Peter 3:9
22. Acts 2:24, 32; 3:15, 26; 4:10; 5:30; 10:40
23. Acts 3:19, HCSB
24. Acts 4:12, HCSB
25. 2 Peter 3:9

Chapter 26
1. Hebrews 12:1-2
2. Hebrews 4:12
3. John 15:16
4. John 16:7
5. John 14:16
6. John 14:17
7. John 14:18, HCSB
8. John 14:20
9. John 16:33, KJV
10. John 16:33a
11. Hebrews 11:1, 2
12. Joshua 1:7, 8
13. Genesis 3:10
14. 1 Kings 19:9, 13
15. 2 Kings 2:3, 5, 7
16. Genesis 12:1-3
17. Psalm 67:1, 2, 4
18. Luke 2:10
19. Matthew 2:2
20. People groups—Samaritans (John 4); Lepers (Matthew 8:2, 26:6; Luke 17:11-19)
21. John 3:16
22. 1 John 2:1-2, NLT
23. 2 Peter 3:9, HCSB
24. Psalm 46:10, NKJV
25. Matthew 28:19
26. Philippians 3:13-14
27. Philippians 4:13
28. Ravi Zacharias, Jesus: Among Other Gods (Nashville, TN:W Publishing Group, a division of Thomas Nelson, Inc.), p. 36.
29. 2 Chronicles 16:9